CONVERSATIONS
ABOUT HOLINESS

BILL & DIANE URY

CREST
BOOKS

Published by Crest Books

Crest Books
The Salvation Army National Headquarters
615 Slaters Lane
Alexandria, VA 22314
Phone: 703-684-5523

Lt. Colonel Lesa Davis, *Editor-in-Chief*
Caleb Louden, *Managing Editor*
Maryam Outlaw-Martin, *Editorial Assistant*
Rachel Domotor, *Graphic Designer*

ISBN print: 978-1-946709-20-2

TABLE OF CONTENTS

SECTION 1: UNDERSTANDING HOLINESS

Chapter 5: Deeper Understanding of Holiness. 79

SECTION 2: HOLY LIVING

Chapter 6: Holiness and Spiritual Formation... 95

ENDORSEMENTS

"The doctrine of holiness is often the 'red-headed stepchild' of the Church. It is overlooked and, most of the time, under-emphasized. The Urys have given themselves to preaching and teaching this vital biblical message. This book is part of that teaching and preaching—fleshed out in their willingness to answer the hard questions. Here, you have the combination of Diane's passionate heart and Bill's careful theological mind, and what they do is unique: get to the nitty-gritty how-to of living entire sanctification. This is a helpful read!"

Chris Lohrstorfer, PhD
Associate Professor of Wesleyan Theology
Wesley Biblical Seminary

"I can think of no one more committed to the doctrine of holiness, nor more adept at communicating it, than Bill and Diane Ury. They have given their lives to this work and in this volume, we see the fruit of that devotion. This reads like a handbook on holiness, every page a worthy apologetic on everything from sanctification to holy imagination to the privilege of singing our theology. Written in conversational style, the text is accessible without being reductionistic, elegant but not impractical. Their teaching moves like hands across piano keys and as they guide us from topic to topic, we can hear the melody of holiness and the harmony of the sanctified life. Throughout, the reader is serenaded by the glorious call to entire sanctification. I am grateful to have this work as a reference and an inspiration."

Rev. Dr. Carolyn Moore, Bishop
Global Methodist Church

"Bill and Diane Ury have written a beautiful and practical resource for all those hungry for a deeper experience and work of God. In this volume, Bill and Diane provide the theological and biblical framework for understanding the depth of God's love and His earnest desire for intimacy with us. This book is an invitation into the experience and life of holiness. Drawing on their deep theological knowledge, biblical training, and own personal love for Jesus, Bill and Diane Ury eloquently answer the most common questions about holiness. In doing so, they share the beauty of this life in God. Practically, they also address the outworking of holy love in the mundane and messy details of life. I know I will be reading and referencing this book again and again for teaching, for ministry, and for my own life in Christ."

Cricket Albertson, Director of Titus Women
Francis Asbury Society

FOREWORD

In a world where the idea of holiness often feels distant, Envoys Bill and Diane Ury bring it close to home with their book, *Conversations About Holiness*. This isn't just a theological book; it's a heartfelt conversation that invites you into a deeper understanding of what it means to live a holy life.

Throughout these pages, our National Ambassadors for Holiness address practical questions from people seeking to understand holiness in their daily lives. These discussions are grounded in real-life experiences and based on clear spiritual truth.

As I have sat under Bill and Diane's teaching and preaching, I have heard them speak with passion and truth, drawing from their academic expertise, rich experience, and personal witness. I have shared meals with them, listening to their vision for Salvationists to embrace the blessing of holiness. And we have prayed together for our Salvation Army. In each of these settings, I have heard their hearts. You will feel the same pulse in each chapter, finding yourself in a warm and inviting discussion about God's best blessings for His people.

At its heart, holiness isn't just about what we do but about a close, intimate relationship with God. Diane Ury beautifully describes holiness as "the physical embodiment of the presence of God." This shifts our perspective from a list of rules to a profound connection with the Divine. It reminds us that holiness is about being set apart for God, belonging completely and exclusively to Him.

Bill and Diane explore the various aspects of holiness, explaining how sanctification is God's work in us, while consecration and surrender are our responses to His call. We will see how holiness is a journey with God, where He provides the grace, and we respond with our whole hearts.

Holiness isn't just a personal journey but one that affects our relationships with others. The book discusses how holiness should manifest through respect, honor, and selfless love in all our relationships. It also addresses teaching and living out holiness in a world of shifting values, emphasizing the importance of staying biblical without compromising truth.

You will be inspired by their guidance on explaining holiness to children and young adults. The Urys emphasize the importance of modeling holiness through love, humility, and forgiveness in parenting. This practical advice is invaluable for parents and educators who want to guide the next generation into a holiness experience.

The Urys will help us better understand our Triune God and how the loving relationship between the Father, Son, and Holy Spirit forms the basis of holy living, providing a perfect model for our relationships and lives.

As we pray for an outpouring of God's Spirit throughout our Army, we will see how true revival comes from a deep hunger for God and a life of holiness. This insight challenges us to seek a deeper relationship with God and to allow His holiness to transform every part of our lives.

Conversations About Holiness is a treasure trove of biblical wisdom and practical advice. It invites us to embark on a journey of holiness, not as a distant goal but as a daily reality. Bill and Diane Ury have given us a gift—a guide to living a life that is deeply connected to God and profoundly transformative.

May this book inspire you to pursue holiness with all your heart, experiencing the power and discovering the purpose of living in the presence of the Holy One. And may the conversations in this book lead you to hear from—and respond to—God's Holy Spirit.

"My heart has heard You say, 'Come and talk with Me.' And my heart responds, 'Lord, I am coming'" (Psalm 27:8, NLT).

Commissioner Ralph Bukiewicz
Territorial Commander
USA Eastern Territory

INTRODUCTION

Since 2017, we have served as National Ambassadors of Holiness with The Salvation Army USA. Throughout that time, we have been offering a session for questions and answers on holiness during nearly every event at which we have taught. Those in attendance are invited to write down anonymously on a piece of paper any question they have about holiness. We felt this would allow them the freedom to ask publicly, in an unhindered way, things they might be embarrassed about wanting clarification on. This session has proven to be the most effective part of our ministry.

We hold every piece of paper on which those questions were written with a sacred kind of love. They are heart questions from officers and soldiers we ministered to and engaged with during meals, private talks, and the Q&A sessions. We can still see the faces as they're leaning in, hungry for answers to things they've always wanted to know. So, as every single one of those hundreds of questions were typed into the computer, we felt such a responsibility to hold them each in honor.

This book contains a sample of some of the frequently asked questions we receive. The printed answers come from our own hearts, communicated in the conversational way in which these discussions occurred. We intend for the book to be read front to back. But we are aware that some people will read only the sections they're interested in. Therefore, some content is repeated for the sake of context. Our answers are short introductions to these ideas, not complete surveys. These are not academic, scholarly answers; they are real conversations with friends.

We prayerfully offer this to you as a resource for what might be some of your own questions. Most of all, we pray that you will gain gracious access to the Holy One and come to experience *why* holiness is beautiful. May you find deep joy and rest in your souls.

In humble friendship,
Bill and Diane Ury

SECTION 1

UNDERSTANDING HOLINESS

CHAPTER 1
Definitions

What is holiness?

Diane:

"Holiness is the physical embodiment of the presence of God." That has been my answer since the very beginning of my ministry in The Salvation Army as Ambassador of Holiness, when a gentleman asked me point blank, "What is your simple working definition of holiness?" I had to answer right then. Since that moment, my answer to that question has remained the same.

It's likely that when we think about holiness we immediately begin to think about our behavior. Is doing this thing naughty? Is that activity good? Is that thought righteous? Our behavior certainly is a significant manifestation of holy living. But it is the outflow of the intimate, real presence of God in our lives. It is not the outflow of our trying harder to be holy.

To say that holiness means "to be separate or set apart" is correct, but that's an incomplete definition of holiness, unless by this we mean that we are set apart from every other thing so that we belong completely and exclusively to the Holy One. Holiness is primarily being set apart *unto* God; secondarily it is to be separate *from* the world.

To understand holiness, we must begin by lifting our eyes to God Himself, who is Holy Love. Holiness is first the Triune God Himself. This personal God exists with no beginning and has no end. God is the Trinity—a communion of three distinct, divine Persons—God the Father, God the Son, and God the Holy Spirit. Even before God created anything, within this Triune Life, there was mutual, self-offering, reciprocal, other-oriented love. That is why the Bible says, "God *is* love" (1 John 4:8, 16, NLT; emphasis added). This reality is much more powerful than the idea that "God is loving." Caring more about others than He does about Himself is not simply the way God acts; it's who He is.[1]

As Christians, I can't think of anything more important than this for us to be absolutely sure about. What this means is that in the Bible—our only authority for life—everything God has said and done flows from His love. All that He commands, even if it cuts against our natural inclinations, flows out of His loving understanding of what is best for us.

God is holy. This means He is the Creator, and His essence differs from that of creation. That is why some people say holy means "other." God is transcendent. But He is not far away; He is distinct from everything that exists because He created it all. Therefore, nothing can manipulate Him. God makes the decisions about what is true. That makes me feel very safe; if I'm confused about what is good or evil, God is outside of my chaos, and He is unchanging. God is faithful and has not left us in the dark about these things. No matter how unsure our thinking might be, we cannot change what He has stated in His Word.

I'll never forget when I realized that God does not make arbitrary decisions about what is good and evil. God did not one day randomly appoint standards for what is truth, justice, goodness, mercy, righteousness, etc. God didn't sit in heaven and wonder, "Hmm. *That* is going to be true, but *this* isn't. And I think doing *this* is good, but *that* behavior is going to be called unrighteous." No. Each quality is *who God is*! God *is* truth. God *is* justice. God *is* mercy. At that moment of understanding, I was overcome with relief. All these character traits I'm commanded to live have their source in the being of this personal God! They're unchanging, loving, and right.[2]

God pours His own nature into the words of His commands. He is the Source from which all that is holy and right flows. His being and His actions are one. What He is and what He does are the same.[3]

When God first created humans, He formed our bodies of the ground, then breathed His life into our body of dust; then the human became a living person. Sin was the turning away from God's life, crawling out of His hands through distrust and rebellion. Since that time, God has continuously been pursuing us to rescue us from our corruption and death so that He can once again breathe His Spirit into our beings. We are created for living in this kind of union with our Creator.

Holiness is the nature and character of God, Holy Love, offered endlessly to every human person, wooing and pursuing us to leave the captivity of sin and self, return to Him, and surrender every crevice of our lives so that He can make His home in us (John 14:23). Holiness is the Triune God of holy love inviting us to live within His very life (John 15).

Holiness is the Triune God of holy love sharing His very nature with us, recreating us once again with His image on our hearts and making us holy and blameless. His commandments are a revelation of His nature and a promise to us, who follow Him, of what He can make our nature become. Not only is God holy, but God's people are to be holy (Numbers 16:3). "Like the Holy One who called you, be holy yourselves also in all *your* behavior; because it is written, 'YOU SHALL BE HOLY, FOR

I AM HOLY'" (1 Peter 1:15-16, NASB). God's desire is not for us merely to obey what He wills, but to do what He *is*!

Holiness is an ordinary person filled with the life of God, living in his or her daily spheres of existence, not merely trying to copy Jesus, but attempting to live a life flowing out of His nature—sacrificially and other-oriented so that the lost can experience the life and love of Christ through us. Holiness is the intimate, personal presence of God Himself, transforming and recreating any person that will say "Yes!" to Him. All of us can become people of holy love.

Holiness is the physical embodiment of the presence of God (Romans 8:9-11; 1 Corinthians 6:19; 2 Corinthians 4:7-11; Galatians 2:20; Ephesians 2:22; 3:14-21; Philippians 1:20-21; Colossians 1:27; 1 John 4:7-17).[4]

Bill:

In a way, this is the most important question a person can ask. We need to be careful to distinguish between the personal nature of the Holy One and the holiness that He alone graciously produces in us. I am convinced that there are only two statements about God's essence in Scripture. One is that He is holy (Leviticus 11:44). The other is that He is love (1 John 4:8,16). Every other aspect of His character comes out of the inseparable relationship between those two revealed concepts. The Salvation Army's entire history and ministry arises out of our God who is, in His very nature, holy love. The amazing thing about the salvation Jesus won for us, and what the Spirit's presence makes possible in us, is that what He is in His nature is offered to each of us through the grace of redemption. Our hearts and lives can be formed by His nature. Life in Christ is to be a recipient of His self-giving holy love. If He indwells, then the automatic result is holiness. But that reception must be followed with bestowal to another. Purity of heart is only true if our hearts are turned outside of themselves toward others. Holiness is the supernatural work of the Father, the Son, and the Holy Spirit in a person. There is only one kind of true holiness: all of Himself in all of me.

What does it mean to be wholly sanctified?

Bill:

This question strikes right at the heart of what it means to be a Christian and to be a Salvationist. What we do with this question determines how we walk with Jesus every day—how we view our life. I have found that often the words "wholly" or "entire" tend to put people off. That is understandable if a person misunderstands what God intends. First, we are not made for a god who demands the impossible. The one true God always provides everything He commands.

This is the repeated refrain throughout the Bible. He delivers us so we can come into a full intimacy with Him (Exodus 19:4). He redeems in order for us to know Him as He desires to be known (Ezekiel 36:23-27). He dies so that we might be made holy (Hebrews 13:12). The only thing He ever asks of us is a personal responsiveness. He wants us to truly and completely believe, receive, and live in a response of love. But even at each of these crucial points, He is the One who provides everything to make those responses possible.

We are never alone in entire sanctification. "Wholly" is meant to include a total response. The Holy Spirit shows us any place where our entire being, our whole heart, is not yielded to Him. Jesus offers a complete assurance that our entire human existence is taken up in Him (Hebrews 2:17). The Father welcomes us as children, not as slaves who can never truly please Him (Romans 8:14; Ephesians 1:4-5).

The key here is to not start with ourselves. None of us knows the depth of our sinfulness (Jeremiah 18). But He does. And He provides all we need to live a life that fully responds to His transforming grace. Much like the language at a wedding, we can speak of true, complete, faithful, lifelong love. Every married couple knows that each of those words needs further work in a relationship, but they also know that the covenantal sharing of love is whole and entire at that moment. We can fully experience a heart that is undivided in love for our holy God. But the only way that can happen is if His sanctifying love is poured into us. I believe that each of us can live hour by hour knowing that Jesus has all of who we are to the best of our present knowledge. What a prospect!

Diane:

Jesus Christ is fully God and fully human. In His incarnation, the second Person of the Trinity took the fullness of human nature into the divine nature for eternity. In Himself, Jesus has brought together what had been severed through our sinfulness. God and humanity are once again united, made whole, in Christ (Colossians 1:19; 2:9). Jesus has come to rescue us from our shattered, distorted condition of being separated from God through sin. He *is* the healing of the wound of separation from Life. Jesus *is* our sanctification. He has come to make us whole.

In the Bible there are many words used for the wholeness that Jesus can restore us to: blameless, peace, integrity, complete, perfect. Each of these words means "whole." But none of these means that we finally have our act together or perform perfectly. All of them mean that we have given our lives wholly to Jesus, and He has given His perfect life wholly to us through the indwelling of the Holy Spirit. Jesus lived a perfect human life, and as the Creator and Redeemer, He offers all of who He is to us so He can recreate us. Only Jesus restores and completes us; and when He does, we are wholly sanctified.

Does holiness mean perfection?

Diane:
This is such a common and great question! The Triune God intends to live with us in intimate union. That is the essence of biblical salvation—union with God; the life of God in the soul and body of a human person.

Catherine Booth wrote:

"All can have this union. Christ, who is no respecter of persons, bought it for us. All through the New Testament, and indeed the Bible, no truth is taught with greater force and frequency than this, that without a vital union of the soul with Christ, all ceremonies, creeds, beliefs, professions, church ordinances, are sounding brass and tinkling cymbals, and all who trust in them will be deceived. This is the very essence of the gospel. Christ came on purpose for us to have this union."[5]

The point at which Christianity becomes anemic and ineffective in the world is when we start the biblical story with Genesis 3. It does not begin with the Fall. Our story does not begin with sin. It begins with a wedding. People were created as the only image of the Triune God ever allowed by God. But human marriage is only a symbol that points to God's full intention for all human persons: union with Himself.

The Bible reveals the desire implanted in every human heart to be reunited with God Himself and to know perfect and unbroken union with Him. He has made us for Himself, and our hearts can never know peace and perfect satisfaction until they find it in Him.

The primary source of every human person's existence, the ultimate need we all have, which is the core of our very good human nature, is to be intimately related to our Creator. He created us in His image, corresponding to Him. We are designed to live in face-to-face, cherished belonging with God Himself—to be His very own treasured possession, a holy people. In the very beginning, before the Fall, humankind was perfect in our *dependence* upon and *union* with God and one another. This is what is meant by the word "perfection" in the Bible.

"Christian perfection" is a life of complete dependence upon and union with God, issuing forth God's love for all people. The biblical concept of perfection does not focus primarily upon our behavior (Are we naughty or nice?). Biblical perfection very simply means finding our completeness in God alone. Out of this relationship, we receive His perfect love for others (1 John 4:15-17).

Sin is the separation from our Creator and Sustainer; it is a result of personal distrust and disbelief in His good nature and character. Sin is, first, willful removal of ourselves from the face of God, His Being. Sin is deciding we want to be our own authority over our lives, that we belong to ourselves. The result of that willful choice is manifested in our behavior.

All humans are born with this proclivity. This is the daily, momentary predicament of our lives. But the One who loves and knows our beings is able to restore and fill us perfectly—not with good things, but with Himself.

God is holy, entirely different from His creation. We call that "transcendence"—meaning He is "other" in substance and quality, and impossible to manipulate. But holiness also includes "holy love." Therefore, His fellowship with humans was perfection of intimacy. In Genesis 2:1-7, His abiding presence, His unbroken relationship, is the "consummation" of reality. Humans are created to live in intimacy with the Holy One.

"Consummation" means "to bring to completion or perfection." That is what occurred in the Garden of Eden. The climax of the creation story is not the marriage of Adam and Eve. It is the presence of God in the midst of all the created order—and with all created matter—especially human beings, who were created in His image with the capacity to bear the living God in their entire beings, body and soul.

The Old Testament word "blameless" is *tamim* in Hebrew. It means to be complete or finished; the state of being whole and undivided. We find it translated as integrity, complete, sound, *perfection*, moral innocence, full, simplicity, or uprightness.

Who is complete in themselves? Only God alone. And even the three Persons of the Triune God exist in mutual interdependence with one another.

In the Old Testament, God's word for describing His relationship to creation is *tov*, translated as "good." It means "just as I intended, perfect in every way." The New Testament word that represents this biblical concept, which lies at the very heart of God's story, is *teleos*, translated as "perfect." It means finished; lacking nothing necessary to completeness; *perfect*.

Paul states, *"For I am* confident of this very thing, that He who began a good work among you will complete it by the day of Christ Jesus" (Philippians 1:6, NASB).

The New Testament call to perfection or completion is the same voice of the Triune God walking in the garden in the cool of the day, declaring, "This is very good! This is exactly what I intended."

Jesus' life and all His teaching and preaching aren't only intended to show us how to live, to be our example, or teach us true ideas and noble concepts. Jesus Christ came to restore us to our intended state of being: blamelessness. Complete oneness with God. Perfection.

Jesus is the second Adam. He relived being human, being *tov* as God intended. Our behavior becomes a natural reflection of His character when we are one flesh with our Savior (Galatians 2:20; Colossians 2:9-10). This is Christian perfection.

As Paul stated, this will continue "till we all come to the unity of the faith and of the knowledge of the Son of God, to a perfect man, to the measure of the stature of the fullness of Christ" (Ephesians 4:13, NKJV).

Why is understanding the Triune God important for holiness?

Bill:

This question has inspired thousands of books, and even after all of that, we are only scratching the surface of who God is and what He desires to do in us. It will take all of eternity to even begin to comprehend this foundational piece to all that exists. So, if we could reduce the major issues involved with the unity of the Father, Son, and Holy Spirit down to the crux and connect it to holiness, what can we take away? First, it is always the Triune God who is at work in Israel. We don't begin to understand anything God does without the three Persons being involved in wooing Israel to the heart of God (Genesis 1:2, Exodus 3:14, Isaiah 6:3). The Trinity did not begin at the birth of Jesus. The three Persons are always revealing that holy love to us. Second, at the appropriate time the Father sent the incarnate Son in the power of the Spirit to redeem the world and to fill us with the love that is the substance of His own being (Matthew 3:16-17, Galatians 4:4-6).

Churches have always attempted to keep the "oneness" of the Triune God from becoming an impersonal force that is so transcendent as to remain unconnected with us. On the other hand, every attempt to talk about the "threeness" of God can end up sounding like He is a committee. Both of those extremes are heresies. What we can say, and it is unique to the Christian faith, is that God's unity is always comprised of three Persons who are eternal love. We believe that the union of the Three is so totally self-giving that oneness is the only term that is sufficient. Is it any wonder that when our Creator made the only image He ever allowed for Himself, He formed a man and woman and their oneness was to reflect His divine nature (Genesis 1:27, 2:24)?

What that means for each of us is profound. Holiness is that Three-in-One God indwelling you and me. The personal transformation that is offered to every person in the revealed Word, the crucifixion and resurrection of Jesus, and the Pentecost of the Spirit poured out on every receptive child of God makes our created personhood meaningful and fruitful. Every one of us wants to know who we are and what we are here for. The shared love which is the Triune Life filling and forming our hearts is the meaning of our entire existence.

Being made in the image of the Triune God tells us that we are each uniquely, wonderfully, and unrepeatably made. But it also means that we, like God, are made for another outside of ourselves. Like the Trinity, we are not true persons unless we offer pure love to another. Love kept to oneself is impossible. Love shared with only one other can become selfish. Only when two in love show love to one another can love be called perfect. There is only one true holiness. Holiness is eternal, mutual self-offering love. That is why being made holy, being sanctified, is not a side issue for a Wesleyan-Holiness denomination or group. Holiness is God's own life made real and made known in a human life and, as a result, in a human community.

If the One who is Holy Love made all that is out of His fullness and perfect purpose, then we image-bearers are to understand ourselves in light of the intentions of the heart of our Three-in-One God. He has made us in such a way that we have the capacity for His full presence in our lives. His three-personed nature can fill, form, and flow out of our personal lives toward others.

What is the "second blessing" work of grace?

Bill:

"Secondness" is a place of loving disagreement in the history of the Church. First, we who believe in a radical change that comes from justification are not advocating that anything the Lord does on our behalf is a "halfway" job that needs a second dose to take effect. Far from it! There is enough power in the sacrifice of Christ and His resurrection to completely deal with sin, death, and the devil. Any further work in a believer's heart is due to a problem on our side, not God's.

No sincere, biblical believer would argue against the blessing of the saving work of Christ in a human heart. However, a careful and complete biblical assessment clearly indicates that more is needed to be done in each of our hearts than an initial deliverance. I wonder how many times Yahweh tells the people He delivered that they are stiff-necked (2 Kings 17:14; Nehemiah 9:29; Jeremiah 17:23; Acts 7:51). It appears that the first blessing of the exodus from Egypt did not change the hearts of those who were set free (Psalm 106:7). This is the same pattern seen in the New Testament. Jesus continually points out the places where His disciples are not like Him in any way (Mark 8:33, Luke 24:24-25). They believe in Jesus. He calls them His friends. But there remains a deep need in each of them. They need something more. It is arguable that the main reason for the writing of most of the Epistles is the sanctification of believers (Romans 12:1-2, 1 Corinthians 12:31, 2 Corinthians 7:1). The Lord of holiness repeatedly clarifies our fundamental need.

Once again, we must protect against any misunderstanding. We don't get "more" in this subsequent blessing. The Holy Spirit does not give Himself with reserve when we are born again and then really bestows the "good stuff" at sanctification. There is no second salvation or half salvation from God's perspective. There is not a caste system in the redeemed: those who flounder and the elite! We are all the same before our Maker and Deliverer.

That being said, how does one move from the whining, complaining, bickering, disobedience, and warped loves that are found in those who have been taken out of the kingdom of darkness but still retain old, selfish patterns?

Moses used a graphic picture when addressing the stiff-necked. "Circumcise your hearts," he advocated (Deuteronomy 10:16, NIV). Ezekiel spoke of a time when Yahweh would come to those who knew freedom but lost it by profaning the holy name of God (Ezekiel 36:16-21). The Lord of holy love promised to cleanse the people from all impurities and from all idols. "I will give you a new heart and put a new spirit in you; I will remove from you your heart of stone and give you a heart of flesh. And I will put my Spirit in you and move you to follow my decrees and be careful to keep my laws" (Ezekiel 36:26-27, NIV). And then, He says it one more time so that there is no mistaking His purpose for all of us, "You will be my people, and I will be your God. I will save you from all your uncleanness" (Ezekiel 36:28-29, NIV). Jeremiah offered a remarkable view of the covenantal law that Jesus underscored. "I will put my law in their minds and write it on their hearts" (Jeremiah 31:33, NIV). Jeremiah says this deeper work is a new covenant, like the old in intimate self-giving, but one which would complete the purpose of the Exodus: to get the people into the land where they could be living expressions of the only Holy One.

Sometimes "second blessing" language can be confusing. We are not looking for a "second dose" of grace to *really* get the job done. The best way to understand this is to be fully honest with ourselves. If there is any place in our hearts, minds, desires, passions, plans, or choices not fully yielded to Him, then a child of God has two very distinct choices: either try to live with that inner, crushing division or reach out in faith and ask the Lord to complete in them what they realize must be done. In the history of the Church, those who have moved into this "second" reality are those who can truly say that Jesus is Lord of all of their existence. That is what eternal life means.

What does "holistic holiness" mean?

Diane:

Holiness is the Triune God of holy love. God is both holy and He is love. To consider the holistic nature of holiness means that we must continually recognize the nature of trinitarian love. God is not a monad, a single entity; God is a mutual relationship of three Persons who continuously offer themselves in reciprocal, other-oriented, self-offering love. God's own completeness exists in mutually dependent relationship. Therefore, the nature of our holiness is other-oriented, sacrificial love—always considering first what is best for the other, not self (1 Corinthians 10:24). That is holistic holiness. We live in community with others, together sacrificially looking out for one another. There's an inter-dependence of persons who relate according to holy, morally absolute goodness and truth, and in deference to the others' needs.[6] That is why holiness is the foundation and stability of all human relationships.

As individual persons, holiness is holistic in that we pay attention to the way our Creator designed us. Our bodies, emotions, thoughts, wills, and hearts are intricately connected. We cannot abuse our physical health by overeating or under resting because that will affect our emotions and ability to live and serve fully. What we think is true affects what we do, and so on. God wants us to be whole. We are complete only when we are fully His. His presence abiding within our entire beings, ruling over us in perfect love, is the only way to experience holistic peace—what He intends for every person. That's why Paul carefully wrote, "Now may the God of peace Himself sanctify you entirely; and may your spirit and soul and body be kept complete, without blame at the coming of our Lord Jesus Christ. Faithful is He who calls you, and He also will do it" (1 Thessalonians 5:23-24, NASB).

CHAPTER 2

DISTINCTIONS

What is the difference between sanctification and entire sanctification?

Diane:

Sanctification is God's self-offering work of grace in a person's life. Holiness is God Himself. Holy Love is who He is and what He is. Nothing is holy unless God is intimately present to it. That includes people. God has commanded us to be holy. God provides the way to obey this command: He sanctifies us so we can be holy. He puts His life into us (Colossians 1:27). Jesus referred to this as being "born from above" (John 3:3-8). The Apostle John writes about this as being "children of God," "born of God" (1 John 2:25-3:10). God's nature is to continuously offer His very life to dwell within us in intimate love.

Sanctification is the Holy One pouring His life into ours through an intimate relationship of love. Every human being who has ever lived is created with a capacity to be filled with the life of this Holy God. When God created the first human, the Bible tells us, "Then the Lord God formed the man of dust from the ground, and breathed into his nostrils the breath of life; and the man became a living person" (Genesis 2:7, NASB). The Breath of God is the third Person of the Trinity, the Holy Spirit. Without the Spirit in our dust-like bodies, we cannot be the living persons God intends for us to be. We know that in Genesis 3, both Adam and Eve turned their faces away from God's face because they did not trust in His holy love. As a result, God's Spirit was rejected; since then, all human beings have been born in a ruined condition, not what God intended. Therefore, we are automatically focused on ourselves in our thoughts, decisions, and behavior. We are trapped in sinful nature.

This breaks our heavenly Father's heart, and He refuses to leave us in this captivity. Therefore, the second Person of the Trinity, Jesus Christ, came to rescue us. He took on our dust-like bodies while at the same time remaining fully God. Like the first Adam before he turned away from God, Jesus is "human dust" filled with God's Breath. He lived every moment of His life in the Spirit and completely dependent upon His Father in loving trust and obedience (John 5:19). Jesus came to recreate us. He tells us we must be "born from above," "born of the Spirit" (John 3:3-8).

What Jesus means by this is that we don't have to remain in a state of spiritual death, which is what sinfulness is. We can turn our faces back to God. The word for this is repentance. God can put His life back into ours. When we are born again, that is what happens. The Spirit of God is received back to His rightful place in our "dust." He "re-lifes" us and makes us family! This is *initial* sanctification. It's like being invited inside your true home after you've been living out on the porch your whole life!

Once we've moved into God's heart, He intends to move into every crevice of our hearts. After we've come to know Him by being born of the Spirit, He will show us that there's still more He wants to do in our lives. Through His Word, we realize that there's a lot of self lurking in the way we're trying to follow Jesus. We are made to belong completely to Him. He invites us to surrender our entire beings to Him. His love for us is so thorough that He will cleanse us with holy fire so that we can live and love in ways that flow out of His holy nature. When we yield all of ourselves to all of Him, God's presence fills our minds, souls, and bodies. This has often been referred to as an exchanged life: all of me, for all of God. The Spirit reveals to us that we are still clinging to the throne of each of our lives. We choose to put that to death, to be crucifed with Christ (Galatians 2:20). The Lord Jesus alone reigns by filling us with the Spirit of Himself. Christ is our life (Colossians 3:3-4)! That is *entire* sanctification (1 Thessalonians 5:23-24): a total mutual self-giving and receiving—our lives for His life! It begins in a moment and carries on with greater love for the rest of our lives, "that you may be filled to all the fullness of God" (Ephesians 3:19, NASB).

Sanctification is not something we do. It's a gift received by faith. Charles Wesley would often write that it is both a gift and the giver. We yield to God's work of transforming our lives into the image of Jesus. This is what we are created for! Fullness of joy and peace will pervade our lives.

Bill:

The difference is quite important. The concept of salvation is a broad one for us. It extends from the heart of God before creation to the other side of eternity. Our holy God intends all those who are saved to share eternity with Him. In a similar way, sanctification has a general meaning. So often in the Bible the people of God are called holy even though their lifestyles may still not be pleasing to the Lord (1 Corinthians 1:2). But the specific call to be *entirely* sanctified (1 Thessalonians 5:23) pertains to a deeper work that God intends for every believer (1 Thessalonians 3:10).

It is at that point that a lot of our debate with other theological traditions begin. Many believe that all we can hope for is a general experience of being called holy without really ever becoming what God plans for every Christian. We Salvationists lovingly disagree. We are holy only because of what God has done for us. But His loving desire to do in us a work that is pleasing to His holy heart is the inheritance of every daughter or son of God. Entire sanctification is the privilege of every believer.

What is the difference between holiness and sanctification?

Diane:

Holiness is God Himself. In order for us to be holy, live a holy life, experience holiness, strive after holiness, we must pursue the Holy One and be filled with the presence of the Triune God. Sanctification is the loving act of God pouring His own life into ours. When we speak of living a life of holiness, what we mean is living in intimate union with Jesus so that His life is manifested in ours (Ephesians 1:3, 11; 2:6-10, 21; 3:16-20; Colossians 2:9-10; 2 Corinthians 4:5-11). We call that way of life "holiness."

Bill:

We always need to be careful about our use of terms that apply to our Savior and the salvation that He alone has offered to all who would believe. Holiness is best understood as that which shares the nature and character of God. Wherever His nature, His holiness is present, that object, place, or person is rightly deemed "holy" (Exodus 3:14, Isaiah 6:3). Sanctification most often refers to the means by which something or someone is made holy. So, the terms are not ever separated, but they offer different and necessary emphases. If holiness describes what

God desires to do in us, then sanctification ("to make holy") is the action required for His ultimate purpose in us to be fulfilled.

What is the difference between consecration and sanctification?

Diane:
When the word sanctification is used, that is always what God the Spirit does. Not what we do. God offers Himself to us through sanctification. Consecration is what *we* do. We offer ourselves to God. We acknowledge that He is perfectly good and loving, so we can trust Him. Consecration is entrusting our entire beings to Him. We separate ourselves *from* every other possible source of reliance and provision—these are idols. We attach ourselves *to* the one true Source of life. This is the choice to fully belong to Jesus. Holiness is belonging! Have you ever felt unwanted or utterly alone? This response to God is offering your entire self to the One who made you and knows the way to live, which will bring you true satisfaction. Jesus knows you perfectly and loves you completely. And He will never abandon you! Consecration includes surrender because it is through yielding up our rights to ourselves that we are then able to receive His presence as King, Lord, Healer, and the One who makes us holy.

The holy life is relationship. God doesn't zap us with a holy-making ray gun. It's not something that just happens to us. Holiness is a mutual, intimate, personal relationship with the holy-making God. Our role is significant because we have free will. We must choose to receive God's loving offer of His presence. And we must surrender to His terms. He is God, we are not. His standards for life are perfect, good, just, beautiful, and non-negotiable. Consecration on our part is acknowledging this, putting to death our self-will regarding all areas of life, and promising to live in obedience to God's Word. There will be no sanctification without our consecration.

What is the difference between surrender and consecration?

Bill:

Surrender is primarily focused on what we offer. To surrender is to give up oneself, to become vulnerable, to acknowledge that one has been beaten, and to act in a way that holds no pride or self-determination. This unreserved yielding has more to do with our will, our own commitment to the Lord. Of course, nothing we do that is saving is done in our own power, so this self-giving is enabled by the Holy Spirit.

Consecration is different from surrender. Surrender might be viewed as a general category while consecration is a particular kind of "setting apart." It is more specifically focused on holiness. In the Old Testament, the word we translate as "consecrate" is often "to make holy" or "to sanctify." To consecrate is to place oneself in a context where the holiness of God has full access to all that He desires to reform, to remake in His image. Our referring to being "set apart" comes from the same idea as to consecrate ourselves to God or to be consecrated by Him (Joshua 7:13).

What is the difference between Wesleyan-Arminian and Calvinist views of holiness?

Bill:

There are a lot of great resources that comprehensively compare and contrast these important but distinct conceptions of God and His plan of salvation. As members of the Wesleyan-Arminian strain of Christian thought, our starting point is holy love. The essence of God is what He desires to see imaged in His children. That means that sovereignty is not where we Salvationists begin. We start with Scripture's clear indication that the highest revelation is His holiness. Everything else that exists comes into being out of the holy love of the Trinity (Isaiah 6:8; 1 John 4:8, 17; Revelation 4:8; 2 Timothy 2:2).

The agreement we share with all true Christian believers is encouraging. Ninety percent of our theology in our doctrines is confirmed by millennia of orthodox Christian beliefs. The most distinctive commitments—and differences—with our Calvinist kinfolk pertain to doctrines nine and ten. Because love precedes sovereignty in our worldview, we have a fundamental commitment to the personal nature of all salvation. At no point does saving grace become mechanical or impersonal. As in any relationship, neither party is forced to love the other. It is always a personal choice from beginning to eternity. Though it is painful to consider, there is the harrowing possibility that a person can back up on their covenant of love and leave God (Hebrews 10:26-31). Any other relationship than that would be impersonal, which is not a Christian view of how persons actually relate.

When it comes directly to how we view holiness from these two theological vantage points, we are committed to the biblical commands, promises, prayers, and offer of a heart set free from all self-will. We do not believe that the holiness Scripture points to in its entirety is only for Heaven. For us, death is not the sanctifier. The personal reality of holiness is the most beautiful thing about The Salvation Army. It permeates the whole of who we are. And even though we might be misunderstood and sometimes maligned for our commitment to holiness of heart and life, we are unmoved in our fundamental commitment to this pure gift of grace. As Wesleyan-Holiness people, we always point to the highest about God and the utmost He has promised, provided for, and makes possible in any heart who seeks Him.

CHAPTER 3
BIBLICAL INTERPRETATION

How can we reconcile that we were created "good" with the concept of original sin?

Diane:

Great question! Doctrine five contains these concepts, and states: "We believe that our first parents were created in a state of innocency, but by their disobedience they lost their purity and happiness, and that in consequence of their fall all men have become sinners, totally depraved, and as such are justly exposed to the wrath of God."

The first part of this doctrine is so important. Do you ever notice a sense of longing deep within your being? We can tell something exists that we desire; we sense we are incomplete without it. My first instinct when I think of myself as needing something, as being incomplete, as having desires and longings, is to think that there must be something "not right" with me. To need seems like weakness, and weakness doesn't seem good. And if something is not right or good, then I feel like it must be a result of my messing up, of sin.

But God created us with need. We are created with desire, a mysterious hunger for belonging. He designed us this way so we would know how wanted we are by Him. It is critically important to know that the sinful nature that occurred as a result of rebellion in Genesis 3 is not the primary place to begin to understand the biblical view of humanity. The truest thing about what it means to be human is not that we are sinful. The foundational truth is that God intended—and still does intend—that all human beings live in intimate union with Him. That's why this doctrine of ours begins with this truth: "Then God said, 'Let us make human beings in our image, to be like us ... So God created humans in his own image; In the image of God he created them; male and female he created them ... Then God looked over all he had made, and he saw that it was very good!'" (Genesis 1:26-27, 31, NLT).

To accurately understand what it means to be human, we must begin with creation in Genesis 1 and 2. We immediately can tell by the first-person plural pronouns "us" and "our" that the One who created humans is the Triune God: Father, Son, and Spirit. The one true God is three divine Persons who eternally live in relationship that is mutually interdependent, reciprocal self-offering love. For humans, to be made in God's image and likeness means that we also are created for this kind of interdependent, mutual love relationship.

> "Then the LORD God formed the man of dust
> from the ground, and breathed into his nostrils the
> breath of life; and the man became a living person"
> (Genesis 2:7, NASB).

The Creator lovingly took the dust and formed it with His hands into a human vessel. I picture this event being similar to when we hold a helpless newborn baby close to our face, and the two of us gaze deeply into one another's eyes. God and the human could see one another's reflections within the eyes of the other. God breathing into the nostrils is about as intimate as it gets.[7] The "breath of life" is actually the name for the Holy Spirit. When God breathed His own life into the dust, *then* the human became a living person. Without the Breath of God within our dusty, needy, physical form, we can never be the fully flourishing human persons God intends.

To be a perfect human is not to be self-sustaining, independent, or self-fulfilling. To be a perfect human is to know that we desperately need to live in face-to-face intimacy with our Creator so that He can breathe His Spirit continuously into our human lives.

God created us as embodied persons. Our physical bodies are "very good." They are not, as some say, mere shells that house our real selves, which are spirit and soul, to be discarded as annoying and useless when we die. We do not *have* bodies. We *are* our bodies, just like we are our minds, hearts, and spirits. Our bodies are the temple of the Holy Spirit (1 Corinthians 6:19).

We are made by God, and we are made for Him. He completes us. Our longings for meaning and love exist because we are created in God's image, for union with God. In love, God designed us to be satisfied when we choose Him, when we constantly recognize we aren't meant to live a moment outside of being knit to our Creator (Psalm 139). We are made for Another.

As orthodox Christians, our doctrine does not allow "myths" to form our thoughts and the ways we live. We are not accidents of chance who do not matter, who are merely physical material untouched by divine reality. We are known intimately by a personal, almighty God who designed us uniquely and loves us more than we know.[8] This is the radical distinction between the nature of the Triune Christian God and every other deity. God revealed this character of His through the Hebrew word *hesed* and the Greek word *agape*. This language was new to a humanity trapped in the sin of self-curved hearts. All other deities demanded servile sacrifice from their people for their own benefit. The God of the Bible reveals that His essence is to care more about our well-being than His own. That is most clearly revealed in His coming from Heaven to be one of us in order to die for our sins. This true love is the basis of Christianity.[9]

He intends to make His home within our bodies (John 14:23). He intends that we will cling to Him in devotion, yielding our entire beings to Him.

When God finished creating, He "saw all that He had made, and behold, it was very good" (Genesis 1:31, NASB). In the original language this means, "exactly as I intended." God's intention for His beloved humans has never changed. The disaster of sin spoiled human nature for everyone who has ever lived. But even that catastrophe never changed God's intention for us. Therefore, "He rescued us from the domain of darkness" (Colossians 1:13, NASB). He sent His Son in the likeness of our sinful bodies and declared an end to sin's control over us. We no longer are controlled by our sinful nature. You are controlled by the Spirit if you have the Spirit of God living in you (Romans 8:3-17).

Are you feeling needy and weak? This is not a flaw. This is "a state of innocency." To recognize this is what Jesus called being poor in spirit, and it's the doorway to holiness. You are made for Jesus (Matthew 5:2).

How should we understand 1 Thessalonians 5:23?

Bill:

I have been amazed over the years by how our Bible translations determine so much of how we view our God and the salvation that He offers. It took me a long time to question some of the perspectives that brilliant scholars have brought to the text. While grateful, we must be careful who we submit our minds to. Most theologians bring their own agendas to the Scriptures. Calvin, Luther, and Wesley had lenses through which they saw the riches of the Word. We, likewise, must acknowledge our limited perspectives. That is why the full authority of the Word interpreted by the Holy Spirit and clarified by His continued revelation through the Body of Christ is foundational to a healthy Christian. This is why it is always good to compare translations.

Our tenth doctrine is unique in the history of creeds. We don't explain entire sanctification; we simply quote what the Bible says most clearly about it. Everything that a complete work of God in the heart means is summarized by the beautiful phrase, "entire sanctification."

The King James Version reads, "And the very God of peace sanctify you wholly; and I pray God your whole spirit and soul and body be preserved blameless unto the coming of our Lord Jesus Christ" (1 Thessalonians 5:23). The consistent theme of the Bible is that the God of saving and transforming grace can produce in us a whole heart. Other translations convey "wholly" as "through and through" (NIV), "entirely" (NASB), or "in every way" (NLT).

What is often missed in the translation is that there are two words right next to each other that have the same exact concept of "entire" (*holo*) in Greek. A straightforward translation of the original language might be something like this: "And the very God of peace sanctify you wholly-perfectly (completely, fully), and may you be wholly-entirely—your spirit and soul and body—preserved (kept) blameless unto the coming of our Lord Jesus Christ."

Notice how powerful that is. God will have nothing less than all of that which makes up our full humanity. Every major portion of our lives is included. But the major emphasis is the work that our Holy One alone desires and is able to perform. The peaceful desire of the God we fought for so long is to bring us into His wholeness, His nature, His life. The love that made us for Himself will only be sufficed with a full response of love born in each of our hearts. He will not settle for a love that is less than complete.

When we make entire sanctification about us or our decision or will primarily, we have missed what God has tried to make clear from the beginning. He does want us to respond, but—like all parts of biblical salvation—our receptivity is merely a receiving. He who is Holy gives only Himself. All holiness is of Him and through Him. When He is given full access to every portion of our being, then He can begin what He alone can produce.

Notice how we can so easily make entire sanctification more about us than about the heart of the Holy One Himself. There are numerous ways in which our preoccupation with giving up or dying to self can actually eclipse the beautiful self-bestowing love of God.

Sanctification is God's will, which is referenced frequently throughout the verses of 1 Thessalonians 5:

+ Paul asks us not to quench the Spirit of God (5:19);

+ Paul mentions the God of Peace Himself as the One who sanctifies (5:23);

+ Paul talks of the Lord Jesus Christ (5:23);

+ and Paul tells us that the One who calls us is faithful and will complete our soul and spirit (5:24).

No one debates the trinitarian reality of God's own selfless love rendered freely to us, surrounding us with transforming grace. Where we get hung up is when we remove our receptivity from the personal nature of God's perfecting will. He is entirely committed to making a life of entire sanctification possible. His will can be made my will every time.

None of us are identical. We each bear His image in our spirit, soul, and body. Only He knows what sin has done to us and where we personally have rebelled against Him. The initial work of making us new in holiness begins when we ask Him into our hearts. It is only after we have walked with Him a while that we see that a "completing" work has yet to transpire. Much like the Thessalonians, we sense through intimacy and conviction that we are not where we need to be. So, we must trust the God of peace, the Spirit, whom we may have grieved by quenching His fire-like presence, and the Lord Jesus Christ, whose power redeemed the world and who will come again to judge. That Source of personal, pure love can be infused into our hearts, souls, bodies, and lives. What belongs to Him, He keeps.

We must be sure that God reveals Himself to us in the language He uses. There must not be a reserve in our hearts that is placed there by any human. We love big words—words like justification, regeneration, and sanctification. But it may be that what the Lord is most interested in is the "all" of our lives, our beings, our hearts. He has told His people from early on that He desires all of their hearts, souls, and minds (Deuteronomy 6:4). The holy-making God has one interest in all of us: that totally unreserved core of our being yielded to Him—our heart. From there, He has immediate access to every other portion of our humanity. The key to full access is that sanctified "center." Once that is unreservedly given to our gracious Savior, He defines, determines, and keeps all which we have returned to Him.

How should we understand sanctifying grace in the context of Romans 7:13-14?

Bill:

As with any passage of Scripture, discerning the context is imperative. We can make the Bible say whatever we want if we separate a passage from its setting. The Spirit has constructed the Word in such a way that we can understand the meaning of passages that may be confusing at first by interpreting passages in the entire book to which the verses belong and then comparing what we find there with the whole flow of the Bible.

For fifty years, I have noticed that many people use Romans 7 as the defining passage regarding our experience of being human at all times, even as born again people. Sadly, I think people take this passage as typical human experience because, at base, they don't want to be holy. They know what that means, and they would rather have an excuse for their sin than live in the fullness of life that Jesus offers.

A more complete view of the larger structure of the book of Romans would generally be seen along these lines:

+ Chapters 1-3: All persons need salvation.

+ Chapters 4-5: All persons can be saved by grace through faith in Jesus.

+ Chapters 5-8: All persons can be sanctified.

+ Chapters 9-11: The Jews need salvation like everyone else.

+ Chapters 12-15: Jesus' saving, sanctifying grace is for daily, real life.

Romans 7 is one of the most helpful chapters in all of human history as a description of the agony of life without a full appropriation of the grace-filled life of God. No one can be exactly sure where specifically these verses are meant to fit along the normal lines of a Christian life. Some say it is life under the Law apart from grace. Others say it is just the way it is even after one is justified, meaning that we never really get to the place of being able to truly please the Lord. While evidence can be offered for these, I think it is placed here as a reminder of how our flesh—life without the Spirit of God—will always leave us in frustration and defeat. It is an honest appraisal of any attempt to limit saving grace by my experience. But Paul's brilliant proclamation of the gospel both precedes chapter 7 and follows it. In chapter 6, he has shown that justification by grace through faith has given every believer victory over sin (6:7). Sin has lost its tyrannical grip on our lives (6:14). As freed persons, we can yield ourselves to Christ as He produces the holiness He intended for us, which is the eternal life He both is in Himself and offers to us (6:22-23).

Then come the struggles of chapter 7. Sin is not merely the actions we commit. The source of sin is in our hearts. We need a transformation at that fountain of defiance. Paul uncovers every single person's heart who tries by their own power to do what they think God requires. I want to do what pleases Jesus, but there is something in me, a barrier, a reservation or hesitation to allow the full truth of life as a child of God to impact every area of my will and life. And the anxiety that that produces is nearly unbearable. How can any person handle the passions and desires of their actual life without the Spirit fully applying the grace of God that is now offered to us in Jesus? It is impossible. We must find the answer to this universal quandary in our actual lives. I love that Paul is not super clear as to where on the "order of salvation" this chapter fits. It can apply to any of us at any time. We need Him. Any dependence upon our ability to obey, to do anything without Him, ends in disaster.

So, the victory we have in justifying grace (Romans 5:1), the reconciliation that has been made in Jesus between us and God (5:11), and the righteousness He alone can produce in our weak but open hearts is already a reality for the one who is crying out in Romans 7. I no longer have to live with my flesh ("sinful nature" in the NIV) controlling me (7:25). There is no longer any condemnation! The Spirit can write in my heart the Law that leads to pure love, and any other means of condemnation has been dealt with. I am truly free (8:1).

It is no surprise that for the first time in the book of Romans, the Spirit appears over and over again as the Person who enables and sustains the real, daily victory. What He desires becomes the heartbeat of the sanctified believer's life (8:5-6). It is sad to think that anyone who walks with Jesus would ever feel like they must settle for a life of despair, hopelessness, and inner conflict. Jesus desires that each of us live as more than conquerors in and through Him (8:37), constantly being transformed by His love (8:39). Sanctification depends on two important elements: a full yielding of all that we are to the beautiful Sanctifier who knows everything about us and a life of self-offering (Paul uses "living sacrifice") that is revealed first as countercultural obedience to Him and then loving sincerely (12:1-2, 9).

Considering Hebrews 10:24, does salvation depend upon some degree of holiness?

Diane:

This is a common question in many minds. This verse can make us feel anxious. We really want to check our motives and be sure we're not like a small child trying, through delicate questioning, to get what they want without actually having to fully obey their parents. Remember, we are created to be holy, so we don't need to consider being Christian as anything less than living with the intimate indwelling presence of the living God.

Holiness is the Lord. If, after death, we were to come into His presence and face Him without being intimately made one with Him out of loving surrender, we would end up in "eternal punishment," as Jesus Himself describes Hell (Matthew 25:46). Holiness is not a high-grade spirituality that is reserved for weird, radical Christians. Holiness is our relationship of loving trust with God. "Whoever has the Son has life; whoever does not have God's Son does not have life" (1 John 5:12, NLT).

I think a common and dangerous misperception about the meaning of salvation and eternal life is that it is us living on forever in an eternal existence. But to live on eternally (a wrong understanding of "eternal life") without being in union with Jesus is actually the very definition of hell! Salvation is not "unending life." Salvation is Jesus, *the* life! "God has given us eternal life, and this life is in his Son" (1 John 5:11, NIV).

God has invited us to live in Him and He in us (John 14:16-23). That is holiness. If we don't experience that by responding to His gracious invitation to shared life with Him, we most certainly will not see Him, because we cannot. Our faces have been turned away unto ourselves and not unto Him. I wonder if this is what Jesus was referring to when He said, "I never knew you; depart from Me" (Matthew 7:23, NKJV). He doesn't recognize us because we never gave Him our face. He wants us to be known by Him! Truly, we do not need to live in anxiety about these kinds of words. They were given to us so that we can know what is true about reality. It's not a game. This is very serious indeed. So serious that Jesus gave His life for us and to us! He has rescued us from damnation and has invited us into His heart. Our home is in Him, beginning today and forever.

How does the Trinity teach us about holiness?

Diane:

A glimpse into the mystery of the nature of the Trinity is essential to teaching us about holiness. Because God is three Persons in one essence and being, God is relational. But the Bible tells us the quality of that relational essence. Unlike deities known throughout human history that live with others so that the others will meet their desires, the one true God, within His own being, is not self-referential or self-focused. God is love (1 John 4:8, 16). The inner life of God is *agape*—other-oriented love. Therefore, the essence of the moral nature of "holy" is always qualified by love that is not self-interested. Absolute righteousness and justice are formed by and acted out as what is best for another, not self. Whatever is true and good exists as such within the life of love which is the Triune God. God alone defines what is true, good, and beautiful.

We are created in the image of the Triune God. When He sacrificially saves us from sin, He comes to dwell within us (John 14:23). His Presence means the moral image of God is restored to our natures. As a result, our choices and behavior flow out of Triune love, love that puts others' interests ahead of our own. Paul frequently refers to this as "walk[ing] in a manner worthy" (Philippians 1:27, Ephesians 4:1). Holiness is the life of the Triune God of holy love filling our lives with His holy love. This changes everything about the way we go to work, think about church, act toward our friends and neighbors, drive in traffic, parent our children, and love our spouses. We're set free from the dominion of self-interest to live in joyous love.

What is the significance of Pentecost for us today?

Diane:

Pentecost is the whole point of Christianity! The Triune God has made us for Himself and intends to breathe His life into our dust. We cannot live as He lives without His life indwelling ours, and our abiding in Him (John 15). Jesus' bodily resurrection from death provides the possibility of our being a new kind of person. His bodily ascension raises our human nature into the dwelling of the reigning God (Ephesians 2:5-7). At Pentecost, He sends His Spirit, Himself, into our bodily life so that we can be His body, the Church (Ephesians 1:23).

The Feast of Pentecost in the Old Testament was introduced fifty days after the exodus from Egypt, fifty days after the blood of the lamb was spread over the Hebrew homes so that the angel of death would pass over. It was a feast just fifty days after deliverance from bondage, celebrating the giving of the Law to Moses on Mount Sinai.

The Ten Commandments were God's offering of Himself through words that are not "cause and effect" rules. They are reality. Like gravity and air are realities we cannot live against, these laws revealed the nature of the One who had just brought them on eagles' wings to Himself because they are His precious possession (Exodus 19:3-6). John and Charles Wesley clarified it best, "The Law is the portrait of who God is, and the promise of what we can become." The Word of God is equivalent to a promise. It never fails.

Feasting at Pentecost in the New Testament wasn't a big surprise because it was a part of the calendar of their lives for hundreds of years. What was a big surprise in Acts 2 was that in the upper room fifty days after that Passover, they didn't just carry on with their ritual in boredom; Heaven broke in! Fifty days after the Lamb of God was slain for the sins of the world—Jesus' death and resurrection—the fulfilled purpose of the heart of God became real!

Pentecost is the fulfillment of God's heart's desire for all people—the promise of the restored union of heaven and earth

(John 13-17). The Promise has come to inhabit His own beloved people. In the Old Testament, God wrote His nature on clay tablets; now He writes His image in our hearts. In our clay, we manifest the treasure of His image (2 Corinthians 2-5). This is God's plan for making Pentecost visible in this day.

The Holy Spirit is sent forth from the heart of the Father and the Son. In the "upper room" of your being, God descends again to make His home, His throne, His nature in our hearts and bodies. He cleanses us, sends us out to the world to see it with His eyes, to be moved with His compassion, and to serve the sin-sick and needy so that He can save them!

The Holy Spirit is God, the lifegiving, fruit-producing stream flowing from within (John 7:37-38). The Holy Spirit is the promise given in the upper room during that last supper before the cross, and He is the promise received at Pentecost (Luke 24:49).

The Holy Spirit was the key to the earthly, dusty life of Jesus. He was the Source of Jesus' life and ministry, and He is the secret, the mystery, the Source of our life. He is "Christ in you, the hope of glory" (Colossians 1:27, NIV).

> "On the evening of that first day of the week, when the disciples were together, with the doors locked for fear of the Jewish leaders, Jesus came and stood among them and said, 'Peace be with you!' After he said this, he showed them his hands and side. The disciples were overjoyed when they saw the Lord. Again Jesus said, 'Peace be with you! As the Father has sent me, I am sending you'" (John 20:19-21).

In just a few days, this was made real.

The first Pentecost was just the beginning. This experience of the Spirit coming in power to cleanse us of self-domination for the sake of others is normal Christian life. It is what we call holiness. There is no holiness for any person without God coming from Heaven into our lives to fill us and make us like Himself.

Love divine, all loves excelling,
Joy of Heav'n to earth come down;
Fix in us thy humble dwelling;
All thy faithful mercies crown!
Jesus, Thou art all compassion,
Pure unbounded love Thou art;
Visit us with Thy salvation,
Enter every trembling heart.

Breathe, O breathe Thy loving Spirit
Into every troubled breast!
Let us all in Thee inherit;
Let us find that second rest.
Take away our bent to sinning;
Alpha and Omega be;
End of faith, as its beginning,
Set our hearts at liberty.

– Charles Wesley[10]

Does describing human nature as "hungry"[11] minimize sin?

Diane: I don't think speaking of human nature as "hungry" minimizes the reality of original sin. I think it clarifies what sin actually is. We often have a distorted view of sin as being something like a physical germ, or a virus. Something that needs to be eradicated, pulled out like a weed. But sin is the absence of the Presence of God. Sin is not our created condition; it's the corruption of God's created intention, the result of our turning away from our Source of life. We rebel against God's authority and don't want His Presence in our mind or body because He gets in the way of our desire to be gods of our lives.

When our first parents, Adam and Eve, did just that, created human nature was emptied of God's moral image. By God's grace alone, humans still have physical life, rational minds, emotions, and free will. But God's moral image is gone. It's lost. Humans are born "lost." Truth, kindness, mercy, righteousness, goodness—all of those are of God's essence. When we turn away from God, we turn away from His Presence and His character. Without Him we are without truth, kindness, mercy, righteousness, love, and goodness. Without God's presence, humans are curved in upon our own selves—corrupt, distorted, deceived, disgusting, and spiritually dead. That's the sinful nature. Bible translations might call this "flesh," "sinful nature," or "carnal nature".

But it's crucial that we understand our sinful nature didn't happen because something bad was *added* to our human nature. Sinful nature occurred because something was *removed* from our human nature—the Creator's loving Presence was rejected.

As a result, our created desires, which were good, are now distorted. We sense this emptiness and try to fill it with all kinds of things to satisfy our longings: money, power, sex, popularity, fame, control, material things, entertainment, etc. They are only counterfeits of what will truly satisfy our longings. We indulge our emptiness, our insatiable appetites with these, but they cannot be sated in this way.

It's interesting to note that the initial rebellion occurred through food, a deceiving invitation to taste of false goodness outside of God's design, to distrust God's goodness. Those who continue to feed on delusion are starved, emaciated people. They are dehumanized by feeding on "trash".

The truest thing about every human being is that we are created for oneness with God, our Source. Every human person's condition from conception is sinful nature—separated from God, empty of God. I'm calling that hunger. It's ugly and it's hopeless, except that Jesus has come for us! He is the Bread of Life, and He tells us that unless we eat of *Him* we will die. But if we do feed on Him we have life eternal (John 6:32-58).

To what extent was Paul's declaration from Philippians 4:11, "I have learned to be content," connected to the idea of satisfaction as sanctification?

Diane: I think satisfaction and contentment are similar. Satisfaction has a rich and continuous presence throughout both the Old and New Testaments. Repeatedly, God promises to satisfy those who love and fear Him with Himself (Psalm 17:15; 63:5; 81:16; 90:14; 145:16; Matthew 5:6; John 10:10). In Hebrew, *sabea* means "to have enough, be full of, to fill up, have plenty, abundance, to be satiated." In the New Testament, the same idea is often conveyed with the word "fullness," or *pleroma*. This means "complete, filling up, fulfillment, that which fills, abundance." You will notice here that the Greek words for perfect, *telios* (Ephesians 4:13), and complete, *pepleromenoi* (Colossians 2:10), are similar in meaning. Ephesians 3:16-19 describes the life of holiness, where Christ indwells our inner beings and makes His home in our hearts, so that we "may be filled to the measure of all the fullness of God." That is what I mean by "satisfaction as sanctification." We are created to be filled with the presence of God. Only He will ever satisfy our lives. Jesus is enough! In Philippians 4:11, the word "content" literally means in the Greek "to be satisfied because one is living in God's fullness."

We must never view biblical satisfaction, contentment, or sanctification as anything other than literally being full of God Himself. That is joy!

What is the biblical foundation for corporate holiness?

Diane:

The Old Testament reveals how God intends to restore all of creation from the ruin of the Fall. God chooses to do this through families who will respond to His call to belong exclusively to Him, trusting Him alone, knowing and loving Him, obeying all His ways and commands. Noah and his family, Abraham and Sarah, Moses and Aaron, Ruth and Boaz, Mary and Joseph are but a few of these biblical families. The primary reality of corporate holiness is the family. Even at creation, God did not begin His dream for human flourishing with government, education, or even the Church. He began with a man and woman, husband and wife.[12]

Some of us come from tragic distortions of what God intended for family and marriage. Still, some of us will not experience marriage at all. I find it so beautiful to remember that Jesus Himself never married, and yet was the most whole and flourishing person ever to live. Paul never married; the Church was his loving family. Jesus referred to Himself as the Bridegroom because He intends to live in intimate oneness and companionship with every person. His bond with us, whether we're married or not, is the one essential aspect of being whole and fruitful. The Church is His body and our family provides intimate belonging. The Church is Christ's witness to the world through our faithful love and obedience to Him.

God promised that He would provide the land in which His people would dwell. What he promised was the epicenter of economic and military strategy and strength. Within this geographical space, His people would live holy lives based upon His own nature offered to them through the Law—a portrait of His character and a promise of who they could become. When they lived in this radically countercultural way in the midst of a violent and perverse culture, all the powerful merchants, religious authorities, and military leaders who had to traverse the land of Israel would have the opportunity to meet holy people. God's holy people were the only hope the rest of the world had to come to know the One True God. This was God's plan of "corporate holiness." Honest businesspeople, communities who cared about the security of women and children, and provision for the poor and weak presented to the pagan world a new kind of life. Everyone else in all the world disposed of these vulnerable burdens of humanity. But God's law made His people completely different.

God established a priesthood—people set apart with God Himself as their only portion. Their role was to bring God to the people and to bring the people before God. They taught and followed God's laws. They instituted God's sacrificial system that would enable the people to stay in right relationship with God's holy presence.

Israel caved into peer pressure. God wanted to be their all, their ruler, provider, and defender. But no, they wanted to be like all the nations around them who had a human king. This broke God's heart, but He does not thwart human free will (1 Samuel 8:7). Every single king of Israel (the northern kingdom) and many of the kings of Judah (the southern kingdom) rebelled against God. They did this by attempting to stay relevant to the culture. God's laws seemed outdated to what most people wanted. The kings changed the rules to suit what pleased the people. They implemented evil economic schemes, which were highly effective, but evil, nonetheless. They also made alliances with godless surrounding kingdoms because they didn't trust that God could defend them from their enemies.

God sent prophets, human beings anointed with God's Spirit, to speak His heart and words into the ears of His people. Prophets warned against breaking God's laws, prophesied God's sure judgment, and promised God's eternal faithfulness and hope. But the kings and the people would not listen. (Read the book of Jeremiah and underline every time "not listen" is written.) Let me be very clear. Everything these treacherous kings of God's people did appeared to be exceedingly wise and practical economically, militarily, and socially. But the recurrent phrase in their history is, "But what they did was not pleasing in the sight of Yahweh."[13]

Micah 1:5 tells of God's sure, catastrophic judgment against His own people. It's coming. Why? Because the politicians in the capital cities are encouraging the common people to participate in idolatry and rebellion against God's Word. Malachi tells of how the priests neglect the worship of God and are personally failing to live according to His Word. The priests are corrupt, so how could they lead the people? They had become stumbling blocks instead of leaders. Jeremiah 5:31 says, "The prophets prophesy lies, the priests rule by their own authority, and my people love it this way. But what will you do in the end!" (NIV). He continues in Jeremiah 14:14, "Then the LORD said to me, 'The prophets are prophesying lies in my name. I have not sent them or appointed them or spoken to them. They are prophesying to you false visions, divinations, idolatries and the delusions of their own minds'" (NIV). Second Chronicles 27:2 records that the common people sinned even though at that time their king was good!

I highly recommend reading the Old Testament in the *NLT Chronological Study Bible*. Make note of the impact of not walking with God with a whole heart by the kings, the priests, the prophets, and the common people. Each group deeply impacts the others. Not one group is entitled a pass for their personal rebellion. In all eras God reveals an individual who stands against the crush of the "rebellion of relevancy"—a common, lowly person like Ebed-Melech, a prophet like Micaiah, a priest like Phineas, a king like Josiah.

Jesus was very clear about any person who damages the corporate holiness of the community, "One day Jesus said to his disciples, 'There will always be temptations to sin, but what sorrow awaits the person who does the tempting!'" (Luke 17:1, NLT). "But whoever causes one of these little ones who believe in Me to sin, it is better for him that a heavy millstone be hung around his neck, and that he be drowned in the depths of the sea" (Matthew 18:6, NASB).

Whatever our role is, and we all have significant roles for which we will be held accountable, we have powerful influence for good or for evil. It doesn't matter if you're a corps officer, brand new soldier, commissioner, parent, grandparent, sibling, business person, politician, teacher, podcaster—you will either encourage holiness, love, and life in your sphere, or you will make it easy for others to live in rebellion against God, unpleasing in His sight and judged according to the light that is rejected.

We must not ease into blaming others. We can't control them. We as individuals must be holy. We must be full of the Holy Spirit of the Living God. We must love and serve our family and neighbors. We must live in complete integrity and honesty every single moment. We must repent of what God is revealing to us as *our own* sin. That is the hope for the world.

How can an object or place be holy?

Bill:

The unfolding story of the relationship between the Holy One and the people who He desires to make like Himself in a holy relationship is expressed in a way that is instructive. Holy ground is holy because Yahweh is there (Exodus 3:5). The Holy One has one express purpose: that His people be holy as He is (Exodus 19:6). In an increasingly intimate way, Israel's holy

God provides lessons in how His presence invites all who will enter into the closest possible relationship with Him. He provides a holy law, a holy priesthood, holy sacrifices, and then a sacred space called the Temple, which had three distinct sections: a place for holy sacrifices to be offered, a holy place, and the most holy (often called the Holy of Holies) where one priest, made clean and holy, could enter once a year to commemorate the atonement of all of Israel's sin. No area of life was left out of influence of God's holiness. In a remarkable vision of the future, the prophet Zechariah foresees a time when even the bells on the horses and cooking pots in houses will be as holy as any object in the Temple (Zechariah 14:20-21).

All of the inanimate or animal things or beings that were made holy all point to the ultimate goal of the educational process of God. He is primarily interested in human hearts and that end is made possible by the sanctifying nature of Christ's self-sacrifice and the infilling presence of the Holy Spirit (Hebrews 13:12, Galatians 5:22-25). The Life of God can be made manifest in our actual human lives. Everything that God does points to that beautiful and accessible life through faith (Acts 26:18).

How should we understand Sabbath in the Bible?

Diane:

In the Bible the Sabbath refers back to the seventh day of Creation. In Genesis 2:1-3, we read that God's creation was completed. God rested from His work. And God blessed the seventh day and made it holy because in it He rested. We know that in Scripture the only way anything or any person is ever holy is because the actual presence of God is "touching" it or them. The first entity in the whole Bible made holy is time. God, on this day, entered from the transcendent realm outside creation into created time and created space. Four verses later we see that God entered into created matter when He breathed the Breath of Life into the nostrils of Adam and made the human into a living person (Genesis 2:7).

God is not a part of creation. He is utterly distinct from any created thing. He is qualitatively different, other, transcendent. This is not a geographical concept; it's an essence concept. God is not far away. He is immanent. We read in Genesis 3:8 that it was God's custom to walk and talk with Adam and Eve in the Garden of Eden. From the very beginning, God has always been God with us—Emmanuel.

The main idea of Sabbath is that God is with us. And God will take care of us, provide for us, defend us, love us, be faithful to us, etc. The Creator, Reigning Lord of the Universe, King of the World, is present to every part of our lives! God made keeping the Sabbath an unchangeable moral law (Exodus 20:8-11) because He desires for us to always remember that He is present and He will provide. God makes it clear that to rely on anything or anyone besides Him is rebellion and sin. That's what idolatry is. Keeping the Sabbath reveals our reliance. We are commanded to keep the Sabbath holy—to realign our beings to the reality that the Holy One who loves us is right here! So, we rest from making our life work. It's exhausting. And besides that, we're not very good at it. When we don't cease from working and consuming, we move into the idolatry of self. We actually begin to think life will not work without *us*! "God can't really handle all these bills and tasks, etc. He's not really God of my life—I am! I'm the provider. I'm the most important factor in my family. My company can't survive without my working. If my kid doesn't play on elite travel teams that play every Sunday morning for months in a row, they won't get an athletic scholarship."

We are commanded to cease from exhausting ourselves through delusion, from playing a "god," from consuming our own lives into oblivion. This is such a loving invitation from the Lord. He's offering a way to experience His loving care physically, mentally, and emotionally. He does this by saying, "Why don't you go take a nap, and I'll handle this for you? Remember, I am here. I love you and your concerns more than you do! I am able to meet all your needs. You're exhausted. Take the day and feast on my goodness. Let me restore your soul." Sabbath is the antidote to idolatry. Sabbath is so re-humanizing! In this regular rhythm we're invited to breathe deeply as we trust in the One who is our rest.

CHAPTER 4

HOLINESS AND THE CHRISTIAN LIFE

Is holiness attainable?

Bill:

It is interesting to look at sin as a "plague." I have often taught that you can tell the character of a people or a nation by the number of words they give to what most interests them. Think about how many kinds of vehicles there are in the world. How many sports there are. How many kinds of food we enjoy. You can tell how different the authors of Scripture are by the varieties of expressions they used for sin. Describing sin preoccupied them because they never fudged on the permeating cancer of the evil in every human heart. Plagues are mainly external horrors. But there is a worse one, and it is internal. Didn't the COVID-19 pandemic help us to see how weak all of us are in the face of an unseen plague?

It is this internal "plague" that the Holy Spirit through the Word unflinchingly uncovers, much like a spotlight reveals formerly unseen crevices the naked eye would never recognize. I know we make fun, due to our inability to understand, of the book of Leviticus. Have you ever wondered why Israel had to ask the priests to come in and see just how permeated their homes might be with plague-like mold (Leviticus 14)? It was a picture of how sin-ridden we and the world are. And it also clearly shows—pointing to the precious blood of Jesus—what was required for us to be purged. Cleansing is a term for outward washing, but purification and purging is what we need. It is that internal scouring and maintenance of a cleanness the

Spirit alone can produce in any heart that desires a moment of sanctifying grace and a daily yielding to that cleansing flow. To focus on one metaphor for sanctification is never adequate, but there are times in life when it helps us to focus our attention on our deepest need. Have you been cleansed by the blood of the Lamb? He knows exactly where your crevices of self-interest are, and He is ready to apply His purifying love at each needed point.

Diane:

"I will walk before the Lord in the land of the living" (Psalm 56:13; 116:9; 142:5, ESV). That idea has become very powerful in my life. The Hebrew translation actually says, "walk before the Face of Yahweh." It means that we can walk face to face with God Himself in this life. Genesis 17:1 records that Yahweh said to Abraham, "Walk before me, and be blameless" (NIV). This walking, living our daily lives, in a face-to-face relationship with God, transforms our beings so that the way we live is formed by His nature. The Bible says this in such a beautiful way—"in the land of the living." Yes. In this life, right where we live.

Is it possible to stop sinning entirely?

Bill:

We will never, ever for one moment stop needing the immediate, personal presence of the Holy One. Our human inclination is fleshly, or what is called the sinful nature. Entire sanctification is an experience of complete surrender and mutual exchange of entire belonging. We belong entirely to Him as His possession, and He belongs entirely to us as our Portion, our Inheritance. He makes His dwelling within our whole beings—heart, soul, mind, body, spirit. This is a relationship of exchange that results in a total transformation. Like any relationship, there is always freedom to choose. We must daily, even hourly, cleave unto Him in humility and surrender. We are always capable of being self-centered or driven by self-interest. This capacity for free choice never ends. But it certainly can and must be modified and continually purged, out of loving, constant intimacy.

We will never stop needing the grace of the Holy One. Any part of our lives that is not in constant contact with our loving Sanctifier will soon be used for sinful purposes. We must also be careful not to equate being human with being sinful. The Lord is able to make holy what we have polluted because He has made us and redeemed us.

Is holiness a conscious effort or something that should come naturally for Christians?

Diane:

Holiness is a relationship of mutual love with the Triune God. We must give Him all of ourselves, continuously. When we do that, He will receive us into His life. He will continually give Himself to us as we continually admit our absolute dependence upon Him and receive His life through specific things we do. Receiving the life of Jesus continually is not natural. We must develop habits; we must have self-control and self-discipline. We must choose to deny self and the world's appetites. This is the conscious effort part. Yes, it is absolutely necessary to make an effort to be in relationship. Too often, we use "grace" as a lousy excuse for our neglect and willful disobedience. That is not okay. Those excuses damage the relationship. In Scripture, there's no evidence of entitlement to salvation.

But when we walk in His ways, participate in the means of grace, surrendering our lives to His reign and His love, He transforms us. We will become like Him because He lives in us and is our life. He provides for us our new nature (Colossians 3:1-15). We will naturally live our hours in love and kindness and patience. Our decisions will flow obediently out of our love and union with Jesus. A life of holiness is not a life of striving; it's a life of obedient reliance and rest in God Himself.

Once you have received holiness, can you lose it?

Diane:

Remembering that holiness is not an "it," not merely an experience or our behavior, colors the way we consider this question. Holiness is a Person. I always think about the passage that pleads, "And do not bring sorrow to God's Holy Spirit by the way you live" (Ephesians 4:30, NLT). Grief, by definition, indicates loss. To be Christian is to be in intimate relationship with Jesus, "filled to the measure of all the fullness of God" (Ephesians 3:19, NIV). Jesus was clear that we must abide in Him and He in us. Anyone who does not is thrown away like a useless branch and withers (John 15:5-6). Can a relationship be destroyed through cruelty, neglect, abuse, and unfaithfulness? Yes, it can be. Holiness is union with God. We have freedom to make decisions that separate us from His loving presence. He doesn't make those decisions, we do. His nature is always faithful, steadfast love. But we can break our covenant of belonging to Him. Without His intimate presence within our beings, there is no holiness.

If ever you're feeling dry and distant from Jesus, don't be afraid! Just tell Him that's how you feel. Cry out to Him with your honest feelings, even if they're despair (Psalm 143). If you've fallen into sin, do the same thing. Run to Him! Tell Him everything. He hears your cries. Nothing pleases Him more than our responding to His invitation, "Come to Me!" (Isaiah 55:1-3; Matthew 11:28-29; John 7:37-38). Much easier than "losing your holiness" is finding Him, the One who makes you holy, once again. After colossal sin and failure, God said to His rebellious, wicked people, "You will seek me and find me when you seek me with all your heart" (Jeremiah 29:13, NIV).

What are some distorted ideas people have about holiness?

Bill:

The main distortion that I bump into is the wrong assumption that to be holy is to be made inhuman, somehow divinely lifted above real humanity. For whatever reason, that unbiblical idea allows us to shrug our shoulders and say, "Well that's impossible. So, it can never happen to me."

Other confused ideas are for those who know they can't escape the word "perfection," but misidentify the reality. Legalism is probably the most egregious confusion regarding holiness. It is the removal of a personal love relationship with the horror of ever-increasing demands of an unpleasable deity. Very few things are as unappealing or as destructive for a witness to the salvation that is found only in Jesus Christ than a person who states they are saved but keeps trying to save themselves through more *doing*.

Perfectionism also confuses what Scripture clearly says. Jesus told us clearly His goal for us: "Be perfect, therefore, as your heavenly Father is perfect" (Matthew 5:48, NIV). Rather than throwing up our hands in hopelessness, we should look at the context. He is talking about love for others, even our enemies (Matthew 5:43-47). We must be very careful not to import any unchristian concepts to holiness. The moment we do, we become pagan. By that, I mean we turn reality upside down. We are a loving, gracious, self-giving people—that is, we are a people of Jesus. The perfectionist has ceased looking into His face. Sadly, that person looks at religion as a never-ending ladder of self-flag-ellating *doing*. Jesus has nothing to do with that. But He can, and does, by His Spirit, produce in each of us a heart that He forms and fills by His perfectly understanding human hands and hearts (Romans 5:5).

Another common confusion about holiness turns the worship-er's focus into themselves. We call this unhealthy and destructive introspection. Holiness is never a turn inward. Everything about the Holy One and what He alone can produce is turned outside of Himself. Consequently, the person who is filled to overflowing with the Holy Spirit is first turned toward others. Sure, there are places that need attention in our hearts. But to be preoccu-pied with those issues puts us on the wrong track. Instead of looking for ways to serve, give, and love, our morbid focus on our sins, weaknesses, infirmities, and missteps actually hinders the very One who desires to pour Himself into us so that He is what flows out of us!

As recipients of divine love, we must fight every wrong defini-tion of holiness and live in the reality of the truth we have in Jesus. He dispels every wrong definition by His presence and power.

Diane:

The distortion that I fell prey to for years was focusing on my behavior as the goal of holiness. I so desperately wanted to be transformed, to have an attitude of kindness, gentleness, and love—especially in my own home. Plus, there were many "holiness people" in my world whom I held up to be examples of what my life should be like, and I wanted to act like they did, to even have ministries like theirs. I went to the altar a hundred times begging God to give me the experience of sanctification so that I would be changed. I wanted to like who I was! All my trips to the altar begging God to sanctify me and make me holy returned empty. I was in anguish. At last, my desperation was enough for Jesus to get access to me. He revealed to me that I had made my holiness behavior an idol. I wanted to behave well more than anything else, even more than I wanted Jesus Himself. He was saying, "I won't give you that unsatisfying experience you're clamoring after. But I will give you Myself, if you will want only Me."

Focusing first upon holiness behavior is a distortion of biblical holiness. God wants us first to know Him, trust Him, love Him, and want Him. Then we will obey Him. He wants us to live in intimate, abiding love relationship with Him, acknowledging our continuous need of Him. He longs for us to experience that He is enough. Christ is our holiness. We will be holy only when Christ's life is our life (Colossians 3:1-17). Our holiness behavior will flow out of His holy love, filling our hearts, minds, bodies, and souls through dwelling in Him (1 John 4:15-17).

Can you share your thoughts on Colossians 2:11—Christ's work of putting off the sinful nature—and Colossians 3:5, where Paul admonishes us to put to death the things which belong to our earthly nature?

Bill:

Space does not allow us to fully examine how often being saved yet needing something more is addressed in the New Testament. Perhaps one of the clearest examples in the Epistles is Colossians 3. We have already been told by Paul that the Colossians are a remarkable, vibrant church of dynamic believers who have been raised from the death of sin into newness of life (2:6-14, 20). And yet, he clearly tells those who have died that they must "die" a second time (3:5). There is something remaining which he honestly believes can happen once and for all. He develops it further in 3:8, telling us to put off all self-protective patterns. And in 3:9, he points to our weakest area. He warns, "Don't lie to each other" (NLT). Deception is the graveyard of any aspiration for holiness.

Apparently, Paul is admonishing a wonderful church, pleading that they choose to go through a "second death." Why? Because we are humans who have no idea how deeply we are fallen. We can't even begin to understand how warped our hearts are until we have known the guilty burden of our sins rolled off our shoulders.

Let me add some important things to remember:

Secondness does not mean that we are all sanctified in the exact same way. Very similar to our conversion testimonies, the Lord does not deal with us all as cookie-cut disciples. My wife's experience of sanctification and mine are incredibly different. But the basic reality is the same. A believer must come face-to-face with the source of sins. That place is always referred to as one's heart.

Secondness is also always a part of the larger work of God's saving grace in an individual's life. There is growth before a second work of grace and most definitely after. We Salvationists have been better than most in singing, preaching, and advocating for this work of God's Spirit. But we have not been very good in connecting that subsequent work to the entirety of the Christian life. Especially weak is our lack of discipleship that allows people to ask questions and get answers in a safe context prior to petitioning God for His sanctifying grace. And, we have not produced small groups for those who have experienced a second work so that they can submit themselves to the loving accountability we all need to continue to grow in grace.

What is the line that separates being holy and being unholy? If you do something good, do you jump to the holy side of the line? If you do something bad, do you jump to the unholy side of the line?

Bill:

I love the honesty behind this question. If I were to estimate how most folks view holiness, it would be right along these lines! That makes it an important question.

I have a friend who shares a similar perception in this illustration. He says that we often act as if there is a line out there somewhere in that stratosphere delineating between holiness and unholiness. And all of us strive to get as close to that line as possible. We want to be holy—but not *that* holy! So, we skirt that made-up line as much as possible, near just enough to escape deserved punishment but not coming across to our peers as too radical, too prudish, too goody-goody.

Many things break the heart of God, but I wonder if this misperception is not among the most painful. Here is all of His creation, revelation, redemption, empowerment, and folks like us are looking for a line that justifies our dalliances with sin.

I don't believe Jesus looks at life in terms of "lines." He is much more interested in hearts. Sure, it is possible to disobey a clear command of God, which is extremely serious. But to view walking with Jesus in the Spirit as cavorting into and out of holiness is a charade of what He offers to us. He defines salvation, not us. He determines the outlines of that relationship of gracious acceptance and love. Any expression of intimate love has long left behind the notion of lines. Unfaithfulness begins far from any "line." The crossed line is a broken covenant far earlier than that last step.

That is why the Lord speaks of covenantal love, of a commitment that precedes our actual steps and thus, guides them. He gives us an unchanging law of love that instructs us at the heart level, so that our footsteps are pleasing to Him. Adultery begins in a heart before it ever is expressed.

Salvation is a relationship of deep, personal, constantly yielded love. There are lines that must not be crossed. But there is a level of mutual commitment that guards our hearts and steps so that we never have to tiptoe in anxious self-possession or self-condemnation. Holiness sets our hearts and lives free.

CHAPTER 5
Deeper Understanding of Holiness

Is entire sanctification instantaneous or progressive?

Bill:

Someone I know once said, "No one argues that God's grace is sufficient to cleanse a human heart from sin. The debate is on *when* that cleansing occurs." I concur with that assessment. There are three major schools of thought on this very important idea of entire sanctification:

First, there are those who say you get everything at once. To be born again is to be entirely His from the start. Everything you bump into is just a typical Christian experience until heaven.

Second, others profess this "entirety thing" is impossible while we are in this fallen flesh surrounded by a world of sin, so sanctification is really an ideal for heaven. All we do now is aspire to be more holy, less sinful, and honest with our debilitating struggles.

Third, our Salvation Army theological tradition goes back to the salvation Jesus preached and that which the apostles continued to proclaim: entire sanctification is a real relationship with our Creator and Redeemer. It is both a crisis and a process.

We are persons in love with Triune Persons. That means that, from start to finish, there are points of radical alteration in the relationship. But those covenantal commitments are never divorced from the past or future. We are not mechanical objects; we are people.

Instead of working through every place in Scripture that verifies this perspective, let me point out a couple of key passages that help us interpret the command to be entirely sanctified. We do not agree with the other schools of thought because they don't make sense with the clear commands of Scripture. "Be holy, as I am holy" is not a future aspiration or an impossible reality (Leviticus 21:8; 1 Peter 1:16). The Lord is requiring something of us and offering something of Himself. That overarching vision of life with Him in covenantal love is underscored by hundreds of specific applications. All of life—work, family, sex, government, possessions, etc.—are to be brought under the direction of holiness.

One could say those issues are dealt with in process, in growth. However, when you look at what really happened in Israel, they were never changed by time alone. The sanctifying God of Israel kept asking for an honest appraisal of why the people of God kept turning away from Him towards other things. What was wrong at the core of their hearts (Deuteronomy 30:6; Joshua 24:16-20; Psalm 26:1-3; Isaiah 6:5-6)? Why did they not love Him with all their being? It was because they had not, to use one metaphor of many, "circumcised" the heart of rebellion in them. Yahweh never says you will grow in more love. He wants a wholehearted, unreserved, undivided, faithful love. Something definite, personal, relational, and specific must happen in every human heart for a genuine, blameless, perfect walk with God. And there is not a whit of impossibility in these commands. God matter-of-factly states the obvious throughout the Old Testament.

Lest we overemphasize our part in this, we must also see that Israel had not allowed the Spirit to work fully in their hearts. Sanctification was never meant to be an experience apart from the Spirit. The inability of the people of God "to sanctify the Name" of God was not because they were in exile; it was because they had yet to allow the Spirit of God access to their hearts and minds (Ezekiel 37:12-14; Isaiah 59:21). When the Spirit would be poured out, then the fullness of sanctification would occur in Israel for the sake of the world.

Jesus never saw the new birth as a growth process. That is what was so shocking to Nicodemus (John 3:5-16). I have often responded to challenges to an experience of sanctification in this way: if you were once dead in sin and now you are alive, would it be impossible for the Lord to deal with your self-centeredness? The beauty of our theology of holiness is that it is never separated from the entire way of salvation. It is almost as if there are two parallel strands. One deals with the guilt, shame, and judgment for sins. The other subsequent strand deals with the source of sins. It is at that place where Jesus is most graphic. "What comes out of a person is what defiles them. For it is from within, out of a person's heart, that evil thoughts come ..." (Mark 7:20-21, NIV). The list of sins that follow includes all of us. What we do not find Jesus ever saying is that anyone must live with unceasing greed or relentless lust. Nor do we hear Him say that we will grow out of these sins. What He is pointing to is an undeniable heart transformation which begins at our conversion but is punctuated by sanctifying grace in a believer who wants the clean heart Jesus died to produce.

When we get to Acts and the Epistles, the experience of sanctification becomes a reality. Many, if not most, of the believers in the upper room realized the reality that the whole Old Covenant promised: a heart transformation in the Spirit. The evidence of that is in the lives of the apostles, which is inexplicably different from their orientation in the Gospels. To put it bluntly, some "thing" happened to them. There is no other explanation.

We directly quote our doctrine of holiness (doctrine ten) from 1 Thessalonians 5:23. This prayer summarizes scores of places where the early church leaders mirrored the same kind of expectation found in the Old Testament. The difference in the New Testament is that they know the Spirit personally. They have experienced His sanctifying power. Not one of the Epistles focuses on growth alone. The prayers, commands, verb tenses, and expectation for all is that a crisis of self-estimation and the awareness of the power of God would produce a completion or fulfillment of what God desires in each of us.

That entirety of a will yielded in a moment is a world apart from the typical excuse of my own complex personhood (e.g., upbringing, background, damage). It is as real as being born from above. It is a baptism of love, a cleansing from the being of sin in our hearts, a welcome to the Spirit to take total control of the motivation center of our hearts. And it is the beginning of an ongoing growth in true holiness and righteousness that could never occur without the sanctifying presence of the God of holy love.

The Army has attempted to balance crisis and process. We have not always done so well. One place of help would be to see how our founders and subsequent leaders have drawn from the rich resource of the Wesleyan tradition. No other Christians, in my humble estimation, were able to proclaim crisis and also offer a remarkable practical theology of process in holiness. Unless we regather that foundation from Scripture and our past, we will not move forward in offering biblical holiness.

Building on this, perhaps I could make one more thing clear here. The emphasis on "instant experience" is never about looking for some feeling. It is only about the nature of the human will in which we show our createdness. The nature of personhood made in His image means that decisions can be made that change the course of life. Whether it be eating a forbidden fruit, worshiping a golden calf, planning the murder of the husband of a woman lusted after, or reaching for a bag of thirty pieces of silver, all of us know that there are moments when the trajectory of life is altered, seemingly forever.

All of us are different. I have never heard two testimonies that are identical. The emphasis on asking the Lord to sanctify my heart is not to tell Him how to act or when. But only to say, "I have heard Your voice and I desire for You to do in me what only You can do. I have no idea how deep my sinfulness goes but I want You to have access to the inner working of my being, this moment and forever." What happens next for you will probably be quite different than it was for me. Let me say, though, that the result of that kind of intimate interaction will be life-changing. And I believe for anyone who asks to be entirely sanctified and means it will find that God will give Himself in such a beautiful and personal way that their life will never be the same.

Do we lift experiences up above everything else? God forbid. But we do not discount them. No one ever grows into holiness. Only grace can change the nature of a human heart.

Is holiness a lifelong journey? Or, is it "once holy, always holy"?

Bill:

I have not heard too many people say, "Once holy, always holy." It sounds very much like "Once saved, always saved," which I believe is fundamentally flawed. I would agree, in part, with your journey metaphor. To it I would add that the journeys of the people God called to Himself were punctuated with crisis points.

We find many places of honest engagement with the fullness of God's holiness. When His glory broke through, radical differences occurred in hearts like yours and mine. We hear "journey" language a lot these days. I think it is right to acknowledge that just moving ahead may not be what God has for us. There are forks in the road, decisions that take us into wandering for decades, paths that skirt far too close to worldly patterns.

The journey the Scripture offers to the expectant follower of Jesus is punctuated by critical moments that alter the steps. The journey can be one of seeking the face of God every hour of every day. It need not be meaningless or cyclical. We are meant to be headed in the direction our Deliverer sets forth. It is possible but only and always by His grace.

Can you pursue holiness without a crisis experience?

Bill:

It is possible to pursue holiness without a crisis experience. In fact, I think the majority of Christians who have tried to live in holiness have gone this route. The Lord is gracious, and

He alone knows our hearts. Our emphasis on entire sanctification is not the only way to heaven; it is not the "correct" view of everything pertaining to the mystery of God in us. To use an incomplete metaphor, there are some theological traditions that have a higher "batting average" than others. Millenia of testimonies prove to us that most honest believers will speak of a constant struggle with the sin they find at the source of all they do. Described in myriad ways, they point to the self, the "I" that they never seem to be able to deal with. Or, more accurately, they don't know how to allow the Holy Spirit to fundamentally alter them at the source of self, the warped ego.

We are not arrogant enough to claim that we see everything perfectly about the mystery of the salvation of people, as complicated as we are. What we do know is that the paradigm of Scripture offers a universal freedom (all of the human person) by a God who is best recognized as Holy Love. Pursuing Him, because of His transcendent glory, will never end—even in eternity. However, we are not too big a problem for Him to solve before we see Him face-to-face.

I read a comment years ago that I have never forgotten: "You surely do not imagine that the power which took Christ out of the grave is going to be baffled by you? That the God who did that colossal, prodigious act of might is going to find your problem too hard for His resources?"[14] I think that is the humble, teachable boldness of the Army. We look at us and see a nearly intractable problem; and then we look at Him and see insurmountable power to not only raise from the dead but to give us Himself with all the beauty of His holiness. We want God to be God in our lives, with no reservation clouding our perception or diminishing His ability to do in us a work that is worthy of His holy nature.

How can we seek a deeper level of holiness?

Bill:

This is huge topic; but without exploring it, we risk missing most of what God has for us.

The first three things that jump out of my experience of guiding many people who are seeking the face of God with all their hearts include the need for: 1) an honest assessment (personal and communal); 2) a realistic but undaunted desire for continued growth; and 3) a vigilance against any reservations to diving in and being open to all that He reveals.

Digging deeper is an apt metaphor for all that pertains to holiness. Our continual emphasis on the relationship between discipleship and holiness is a crucial starting point. It normally is in the context of refreshing self-sharing and vulnerability that true holiness can be made known. There is no guarantee of truth just because a group of disciples commit to share their hearts. I was in a group for years with men I wanted to be like. We shared intimately and deeply, I thought. Soon after leaving that context, I found that one left his wife and daughters to live a homosexual lifestyle. Another engaged in pedophilia and left a train of broken persons and families. Another man's wife came to me and begged me to help their marriage from disintegrating.

The place of mutual encouragement never replaces personal integrity. You will only grow as you dig into the full meaning of holiness. That means you will find one experience is followed by others demanding significant obedience. The digging in our hearts is what the Holy Spirit does when we really mean what we say at entire sanctification: "Lord, have Your way in me." He takes that kind of prayer very seriously.

When people say to me that our focus on entirety doesn't sound so "entire," I have to disagree. The God of sanctifying grace will not deal with the heart issues that remain in the complex of the human psyche if there is not an unqualified submission to His searching of our hearts. Digging deep starts with an agreement with a divine excavator.

If you find a small group of people who are serious about a no-holds barred relationship with Jesus, you have found an immeasurable treasure. Digging into the Word is an absolute necessity. What I have found is that there is a level of interpretation that comes out of a communion of sold-out disciples. Prayer should show the marks of increasing intimacy with the Lord Jesus in the Spirit to the glory of the Father. Petition is wonderful, but every aspect of prayer should be explored. A significant part of every day should be spent in the presence of the One who is love.

"More, Lord, more" should be the prayer of the one who is digging for the treasure of all treasures: the very heart of God. There is no holding back, no game-playing, no negotiation with God. There is no "arrivalism" or condescension in the one who is seeking after pure love. Every area of life is to be brought into the scope of the full splendor of holiness.

Digging in to seek the Holy One carries with it beautiful costliness. I remember hearing a speaker say once that if each of us were to have a screen upon which could be shown to God and to others what we were really thinking about, it would reveal an R-rated mind. I have thought a lot about that. I don't think that is what the Lord has for us. Scripture says, if He is given full access, He can cleanse us at the conscience level. I think that applies to lust, to desires for retribution, to envy, and even to self-pity. Digging into the Holy One is not for the faint of heart. But what freedom it brings to those "who fear nothing but sin, and desire nothing but God."[15]

Why don't we just live a holy life if we have been made holy through Christ?

Diane:

This question is not only remarkably transparent and healthy to ask, it is the crux of the entire subject. The word "crux" gets to the point because that word means "cross." Jesus was absolutely clear about what must take place in order to belong to Him:

> "Then he said to the crowd, 'If any of you wants to be
> my follower, you must give up your own way, take up
> your cross daily, and follow me. If you try to hang on
> to your life, you will lose it. But if you give up your
> life for my sake, you will save it. And what do you
> benefit if you gain the whole world but are yourself
> lost or destroyed? If anyone is ashamed of me and
> my message, the Son of Man will be ashamed of that
> person when he returns in his glory and in the glory of
> the Father and the holy angels" (Luke 9:23-26, NLT).

To take up one's cross daily was an excruciating prospect for first-century Jews. (The root of "excruciating" is also "cross.") In verses 21-22, Jesus had just told them that being the Messiah means terrible suffering, rejection, death, and—yes—to be raised again. Crucifixions were shaming. They were disgustingly horrific tortures in a completely public, exposed, radical form of humiliation. Corpses on crosses lined many highly traveled roads in Palestine.

To accept that this kind of painful, humiliating death to self is required of every person who wants to belong to Jesus is exactly the doorway to holiness. Self-protection, self-absorption, self-pity, unforgiveness, selfish ambition, self-righteousness—all of it, Paul tells us, must be put to death (Romans 8:13; Colossians 3:1-17; Galatians 2:20, 4:15, 5:24, 6:14).

But there's an exchange! We give all that garbage to Jesus, and He, in turn, gives us every bit of His life in fullness through His Spirit! If we live His life in this world, we certainly will suffer rejection and abuse. The apostle Peter gives us a phenomenal epistle on how to live this cross-life, following in Jesus' steps. It seems like all of 1 Peter is a manual on how to suffer in a life crucified to self and filled with Jesus. Hebrews 11:1-12:4 is another magnificent encouragement.

The key to wanting to be holy is wanting Jesus Himself. Peter tells us that this results from more than intellectual understanding. He would know. He's the one who got an A+ on the question, "But who do you say that I am?" "You're the Messiah!" But then He corrected Jesus about this whole idea of suffering and death. Peter wanted a Christianity that made him a popular influencer. Jesus told him that's demonic (Mark 8:29-38).

After Peter was filled with the Spirit at Pentecost, he became an entirely different person—he had died to self. Jesus was his life. He writes to the scattered faithful, "Like newborn babies, you must crave pure spiritual milk so that you will grow into a full experience of salvation. Cry out for this nourishment, now that you have had a taste of the Lord's kindness" (1 Peter 2:2-3, NLT).

We must hunger for Jesus Himself. We must taste and see that He is good. There are unspeakable joys for those who find refuge in Him while dead to self-interest (Psalm 34:8).

The holy life hinges entirely upon our knowing Him through experiencing His actual life, so that we cannot consider anything else as worthy to cling to—including our own life (Psalm 63:1-8; Philippians 3:7-11). This life is available. Come to that crossroad and taste the freedom from self-interest and fullness of satisfaction—what you are created for! This is a choice of one's will. He's so kind, He will help you. Just do it.

How do I know that I am fully holy?

Bill:

First John has been for us one of the key places describing the assurance of salvation. It is an amazing thing to be absolutely sure that I am a Christian. John says that if I am willing to obey the Lord with all my heart, if I am able to see that His love is forming my response to every person in my life, and if I have placed every ounce of who I am into Jesus as the Son of God and Son of Man, then I know, beyond a shadow of a doubt, that I am a Christian.

Sadly, too many in the Church are caught in a horrible dilemma. They believe that they are redeemed by the blood of Jesus, but they are told in a thousand ways that they are still sinners at the core of their being. That inner conflict affects everything in the Christian life. If a person cannot be "fully holy," then spiritual apathy occurs, depression can set in, and often moral chaos appears.

The marks of faith, hope, and love are sure ways of discerning if a person is living in the light of Christ's love. But an honest self-appraisal by any believer is that these marks are often mixed with pride, self-will, and spurts of anger, or dalliances with lust.

That is where the beautiful biblical concept of entire sanctification begins to make real sense. He has made a way for us to be holy in Him, and that includes the personal awareness and appropriation of what you have described as being "fully holy."

First, salvation is always by grace through faith (Ephesians 2:8; Acts 26:18). Being fully what God intends and offers never becomes a matter of our ability, goodness, or maturity.

Second, holiness is the purpose of all of Scripture, all of Israel's history, all of the life, death, and resurrection of Jesus (Leviticus 11:44; Hebrews 13:12; Revelation 22:11). It is important to make the saving goals of God our own. Our responsibility is to lovingly trust in His ability to do what He desires (Deuteronomy 30:6).

Third, to be fully holy is to have laid down every aspect of our hearts that has the potential of producing pride or self-will. That repentance as a believer is crucial to the receiving of the promised Holy Spirit (Acts 11:16; Romans 12:1; 2 Corinthians 7:1). Unless we allow the third Person of the Trinity to do His full work in our hearts, we will never know anything of true holiness.

Fourth, to be fully holy is to live in Christ. That life began when we were born again but it is a relationship that must allow His cleansing, purifying, sanctifying life to permeate all of our life at this moment and in each successive moment.

Fifth, the fruit of holiness will be a clear witness to our hearts that God is fully pleased with our responsiveness to Him. The Holy Spirit will bring assurance of full salvation when He determines for that confirmation to occur (Romans 8:15-17; Hebrews 6:11, 10:22). The flood of perfect love that sanctification entails means that every avenue of receiving the life of God will be a potential access point of grace—all spiritual disciplines, all aspects of sacramental living, any form of outward ministry that the Spirit indicates.

Sixth, the sanctified, fully holy believer is always devoted to others in love. This is a mark above all others. The witness of entire sanctification is that the Spirit has cleansed our hearts to the place where seeking another's well-being supersedes our own (2 Corinthians 5:15-16). This devotion must include a lifetime of radical accountability in order to retain fundamental openness to God through His body. Jesus modeled for us the relationship that engenders Christian life from beginning to end: discipleship.

SECTION 2

HOLY LIVING

CHAPTER 6
Practical Holiness

What are steps I can take daily to live a holy life?

Diane:

"Spiritual discipline" is a phrase that describes how to live continually in an intimate face-to-face relationship with God. God's heart is our true home (Psalm 84), and He intends to make His home in us (John 14:23). Jesus calls that abiding (John 15:1-11). We don't want to neglect our relationship with Him, or especially to reject Him. If we do, we will return to sinful, lifeless captivity (John 15:6).

God has created our bodies so that they can help us to continue living in ways that keep us yielded and intimately related to Him. The neuropathways in our brains that have been captive to sinful ways can be retrained through new habits: Bible reading, prayer, small groups, Sabbath-keeping, etc. John Wesley called these habits the "means of grace" because they create pathways for us to receive from God.

Sanctification is the life of God in our whole beings. It is not merely a way of living; it is God Himself living in us. Our culture constantly tries to distract us from our intimate dependence on God. Don't be deceived; spiritual disciplines are absolutely necessary for living a sanctified life. Stay focused on the who, what, and how of holiness:

+ The *who* of holiness is the Triune God of holy love.

+ The *what* of holiness is God's presence in our lives, His character lived out through us.

+ The *how* of holiness is life habits that create ways for us to stay face-to-face with God, so He can breathe His Spirit continually into our beings.

You are created for intimate belonging with God. Make space in your days for lifting up your face to Him so He can breathe His life into your soul (Psalm 143).

What are the necessary steps towards effective holy living?

Bill:

Let me enumerate some key steps toward appropriating the inheritance of every child of God, holiness in both the heart and life.

1. *Vision.* Over the years I have found this to be a crucial element in moving forward into the fullness of salvation. We must allow the Holy Spirit to form our perception of what is real, what is actual when He has complete control. Instead, we have been trained to think at the least common denominator when it comes to what God desires to do and can do in us. When a person begins to truly perceive the power of the promise/fulfillment pattern in Scripture, which issues out of the heart of the Holy One for anyone who earnestly desires His best, they see God's promises for holiness of heart are true (Exodus 19:6; Deuteronomy 30:6; Psalm 86:11; Jeremiah 30:33-34; Zechariah

13:1-2). His vision for every believer is that they would be recreated by the Spirit in their hearts so that the black hole of self-centered idolatry might be reversed into a personal reservoir for the cascade of divine love (Matthew 5:6; Luke 11:13; John 17:17-19; Acts 7:60; 2 Corinthians 5:14-15).

2. *Believe.* When followers of Jesus are totally willing to allow their Savior to define salvation, there is an immediate confrontation with the final spiritual battlefield, the will. Believing for sanctification goes deeper than perceiving it is possible. This is a comprehensive yielding in conviction of any remnant of self-will, confession at the deepest place of all masking sinfulness, which climaxes (and each of us experiences that differently) with a "universal yes" to Jesus. Here, the totality of person is included in a level of trust unknown before. All reservations, excuses, and hypocrisies are given over to the One who knows what we personally need.

3. *Receive.* It is here that the initial regeneration a believer has known provides a clear outline of what might be called the second "platform" of salvation. All of this was resident in the heart of the Triune Holy One, revealed in Christ and His glorious redemption and proffered by the Holy Spirit. The entirety of sanctification has to do with our misunderstanding, not any deficiency in what has been won for us in Christ. Just as we repent, believe, and receive in coming into the life of Christ, there is an "evangelical" repentance, a believer's total trust, and a disciple's comprehensive yielding of all that can be comprehended about the "self." This reception is not based on a person's maturity, ability, or fundamental goodness. It is, for the first time, an all-encompassing agreement with the full intentions of the One who has drawn that heart to Himself.

4. Here are a few key things to *continue* in the sanctified life:

Share. Even though everything will fight against this outflow of a purity, which God alone can produce, it is important to acknowledge what the Holy One is doing in your life. This is healthy in two ways. First, it puts all holiness in perspective. He is the Holy One in us. It is to His glory that any sanctification occurs. Second, there is an element of accountability that is resident when speaking forth the beauty of heart holiness. Few will testify to an experience that is not real for very long. Sanctification is not part of a check-off list for the Christian. It is the goal of God for His people that precedes creation and extends into eternity. Speak of His glory that dwells in your heart and life.

Surge. All of the ways that holy people have deepened in their love for the Triune God are to be used at this point of our walk with Christ as well, only more passionately. The Word, prayer, sacramental living, and various spiritual disciplines are all necessary in living out holiness. The difference here is that they are not arduous burdens to be borne or merit badges to be paraded. These avenues of the life of God become the love language between the One who is holy and the one who is remade in the image of God in true righteousness and holiness.

The key to maintaining holiness when an individual begins to explore the deeper things of God is relating to other believers who are willing to band together to seek all that the Holy One has for them. The forces of evil are undone when a person joins with others in mutual, loving, radical accountability. That is the place where all facades are confronted and dealt with. No one is meant to live out holiness alone. No one can grow in holiness alone. If a person says they are sanctified and they have no other person to whom they are accountable, they are lying.

Serve. All that sin did in us to form the quicksand of self is met by the revolution of love that erupts in a person's heart and life. Though the balance of loving God, self, and others is an ongoing area of growth in grace, it is a mark of the sanctified heart that others' needs become of paramount concern. The overflow of the love that binds the Trinity together is expressed in offering oneself for the redemption of those nearest, of those who are most needy.

What can I do to understand the Bible better?

Diane:

There isn't a shortcut that will help you understand the Bible better. You just have to dive in and read it. Sometimes I think about how people tend to read the Bible and wonder if they'd use that method with any other story. Would we fast-forward through a movie on Netflix until we're three-quarters of the way to the end and begin there? Would we then watch for fifteen minutes, go back to that starting place, and watch it again, repeating this pattern twenty-five times in a row? And never go to the beginning to see how that part of the story fits in with the whole? I don't think so!

Here are some tips:

1. Get the *NLT Chronological Life Application Study Bible*.[16]

- Read for thirty minutes a day, every day. You'll finish in 144 days! And you'll be getting the flow of the narrative. Plus, you'll begin catching on to some recurrent themes.

- Write down those themes, ideas, and cause-and-effect situations that you notice are repeated throughout.

- The next time you read that Bible, take your time, read the charts, and study the maps. Take notes.

2. Don't read things about the Bible until you've read the *actual* Bible so that God can speak to you!

- Reading commentaries and other helpful material is fine, but it's pre-digested. The author has received all the nourishment and is just telling you about how great it tasted.

- God wants you to feast on Him through His Word, personally.

3. When you've already read the Bible for yourself a couple times, here's a great book to add to your study: *What the Bible is All About* by Dr. Henrietta Mears.[17]

How can we follow Christ's model of holiness to develop holiness in our own lives?

Diane:

Holiness is not a model or a great plan or design for life. Holiness is a Person. Christianity is not a religion of imitation. Christianity is impartation; it's participation. Jesus is God who partook of human nature when He was conceived in His mother's womb. "Therefore, since the children share in flesh and blood, He Himself likewise also *partook* of the same ..." (Hebrews 2:14, NASB; emphasis added). Jesus never asks us to copy His behavior and imitate His example *until* He has poured His own life into ours through His Spirit (Romans 8:1-17).

We can rest upon His promises. Christian holiness is not supposed to be a struggle of self-effort. Jesus desires to take up residence in our hearts and become the Recreator of our new nature and Enabler of newness of life. "Through these he has given us his very great and precious promises, so that through them you may *participate in* the divine nature, having escaped the corruption in the world caused by evil desires" (2 Peter 1:4, NIV; emphasis added). This is way bigger than copying His example. He wants us to be one with Him so that He lives in us and through us (Colossians 3:1-11).

How can we practice Sabbath biblically, effectively, and practically?

Diane:

I think going to bed earlier was one of the most helpful things to me. That way, I could get up earlier. It was the only way I could spend any time in the Word. At night I was too tired. I'd just fall asleep.

Perhaps our screentime is consuming our schedules way more than we realize. Get your social media off your phone. Leave your television/computer off. Everyone has twenty-four hours in a day. It's up to us to organize those hours into what is most important.

If you don't have kids, Sabbath could look like this:

+ Sundown: Get off your devices—no email, no social media; enjoy a favorite meal, alone or with others.

+ Next morning: Sleep in, spend leisurely time in prayer and the Word, and eat a luscious breakfast.

+ Afternoon: Do a puzzle, read poetry, go kayaking, hiking, biking, etc.

Do whatever fills your soul and does not deplete it.

For those who do have children, practicing Sabbath will probably take more forethought and creativity. It also requires discipline. Figure out what evening and following day are conducive to your life schedule. Do your errands and household chores regularly through the week so they're not "whining" at you from the laundry room on your Sabbath.

Your work can be ordered and energetically accomplished through other days of the week. Sometimes you'll have to fight for your day to Sabbath. Some weeks you'll realistically have to move your Sabbath around.

Here's what one family with four young kids does:

+ Sundown: Turns off phones; has family movie night with pizza.

+ Next morning: Dad, who normally has less time with his kids during the week, makes breakfast and spends hours doing something with the kids. Mom rests, reads, journals, etc. Family has devotional time together with each child participating.

+ Afternoon: Hikes, or friends come over for dinner or a picnic.

Do whatever is restful and restorative for you.

Don't be worried or legalistic. Sabbath is a word from the Lord, and it is a gift from His heart to reveal His kindness and goodness. Receive it that way.

Interestingly, you will absolutely discover that you are more alive and more full of energy and ideas the day after your Sabbath than any other day. You (and your family) will love the healing peacefulness from not racing around. Alone or together, embrace being home or with friends, reading, playing, and eating awesome food—all of which are symbols of the presence of our good God.

How can parents make time for Jesus in their busy lives?

Diane:

Spending time with Jesus must be your first priority. If your spouse and kids know that, it is a blessing in their lives! Children know if their parents are reading their Bibles, and that forms their minds and hearts. My toddler son used to get up early while I was having quiet time, so I just plastered him across my chest with his legs around my waist. I read out loud instead of silently. Little did I know how deeply he was listening until one time he whispered into my neck, "Mommy, read it again." Older kids can learn to leave you alone until you're finished. When they see that's a priority, that they're not the center of the universe and Jesus is, that's really good for them!

How do we attain that degree of holiness in which we can have the constant companionship of the Holy Spirit?

Diane:

I think if you just rearrange this question, you're on the right track! "The constant companionship of the Holy Spirit is holiness." This most precious friendship must be nurtured through time spent together, and attention given to Him to listen to His Voice. Write down what He says. Obey every word. Pray to the Holy Spirit. He's our personal God, every bit equal to God the Father and God the Son. Speak with Him. Pour out your heart to Him. Ask Him for wisdom, guidance, love, and patience. Practice acknowledging His loving presence and care for you.

What does self-denial look like in practical ways?

Bill:

I have spent a lot of time trying to understand what Jesus meant by the command to His disciples that you "must deny yourself" (Mark 8:34; Matthew 16:24). It fascinates me that Mark uses the word "deny" in only one other chapter in his Gospel—in chapter 14, when Peter denies Jesus three times. If we compare the usages of the term, it sheds light on just how radical this call of Jesus is to everyone who claims to follow Him. It means that I refuse to find my identity in myself. I must be willing to "disown" or put an end to dependence on myself. It is to say "no" to me, in the sense of trying to live out of a relationship with myself at the center. And it would mean that I cut off any self-interested love.

One of the reasons I believe a person can be sanctified in a moment is because Jesus uses a tense in the verb "deny" that indicates it must happen in a moment with the implications of that decision affecting all that comes after. I love that Luke includes another thrust of Jesus that we are to "die daily" (Luke 9:23).

The practical nature of this call to die to oneself is remarkable in what follows. Jesus never takes salvation or holiness into the spiritual stratosphere. For Him, it always touches the next thing nearest our hearts. The first thing Jesus points to is not hoarding yourself. The word "life" (*psychē* in Greek, used four times in Mark 8:35-37) can mean physical life as well as the central spiritual reality of personhood. We must not keep any portion of our actual life from His touch. He must have absolute access at all times to whatever we may think brings us our identity.

Second, Jesus shifts right into the material aspects of life. Most often we define self by what we have gained. When you think of profit and loss, what comes to mind first? Jesus is the Creator. He is not bashing material things. What He is pointing out is that when we don't deny a physical thing to which we might attach ourselves, it immediately becomes an idol. We are created to only attach ourselves to Him.

Third, Jesus then moves beyond the typical areas where we fight denial of ourselves to one that incorporates Him in our daily life—a life in which those who surround us seem to be doing quite well without Jesus. Being ashamed of Christ occurs when we attempt to protect ourselves by not admitting our absolute dependence on Jesus. In this increasingly materialistic and rationalistic world, it is very hard to overtly testify to casting ourselves in unreserved, passionate, subservient love to an unseen Lord whom we claim is Master of our lives. Try to testify to that reality anywhere outside your corps. You will find out pretty quickly whether you are ashamed of Christ or not.

In all of these aspects of self-denial, we must be careful not to overemphasize ourselves! Oswald Chambers has helped me for decades of being made a disciple of Jesus. The year I was sanctified, I read his insightful statement, "The Spirit must enable us to sanctify our sanctification."[18] In the passages regarding self-denial, Jesus is asking us to define who He is. Could it be that giving up the self is the very nature of holiness? Is Jesus not merely correcting bad theology but instead offering us an insider's look into the very heart of God, the meaning of atoning grace, the beauty of a heart set free of self-provision?

What does it look like to live out the definition that "holiness is purity of love"?

Bill:

There are some expressions of holiness that seem to transcend others, or at least, encapsulate them. John gives us that world-altering description of the life of the Trinity as the God who is love. From that nature, we find our ultimate fulfillment as those who are made to image that love. We are to be the recipients and expressions of "perfect love" (1 John 4:16-18). Use of the word "purity" in this question highlights the need for a profound decontamination at the heart level. We can be redeemed Christians and still be unable to give and receive love as we ought.

There are two aspects of love in which we need the purifying touch of the Holy Spirit. The first has to do with our inability to receive love because we are suspicious of the motives behind that love. We are so used to loving for something in return that we impose that selfish intention on love offered to us. If it is hard for you to receive love, then there is a high probability that you need the refining work of the Spirit.

The second indication of the need for a purging work results from our withholding of love. If you are not a free (and personal) channel of the love that is God's own Life, then there is a dam somewhere in your being. We do not give love because we feel the object of our love is unworthy or because we fear they will reject our love. Those judgments, and their resultant reservation, point to a constitutional flaw that needs recreative mending.

It is clear from the context of 1 John that there are some basic tests for this kind of love. We need to be so enraptured by the love of God, which is His nature, that obedience to His command to love comes prior to any of our well-reasoned hesitations. Perfect love is a love that is shared with those who "deserve" it and those who don't—without favoritism.

Also, love consists of more than mere emotion or passion. It is *agape* love, which we know is the love shared between the persons of the Trinity. It is that love that is poured into our hearts (Romans 5:5). So, especially with a reality as divine as perfection in love, we must aspire to comprehend the meaning of the exchanged life. Without the Holy One perfecting the love in our loveless or reserved hearts, there is no hope of that love forming our attitudes and actions.

Note the emphasis in 1 John 4:16-18 on fear. Perfect love always removes unholy fear of any kind. We have mentioned the fear to love, but without receiving and offering the love that is sourced in the Trinity, we will be filled with all sorts of ridiculous dreads. Love dispels the fear of rejection, of losing reputation, of insufficient funding, of being recognized. I would challenge you to find one thing in all of life that can stand against or defeat perfect love. There is not one. It is eternal and a real thing that can be made known in any believer's life.

What are some practical steps we can take to become more aware of the power of God's grace in our lives?

Diane:

It's always most helpful first of all to remember what grace truly is. Grace is not a thing. Grace is not a force or a power. Grace is the graciousness of God's heart toward us in giving Himself to us. Always think about biblical ideas within a personal paradigm. Everything about Christianity is personal relationship.

So, you're correct! Grace is way stronger than sin is. Jesus is the One who reigns over the entire universe, including our hearts. When we surrender all of ourselves to the King and receive Him into our lives, He reigns over our sinful natures (Romans 8:1-17). But remember, this is a relationship, not merely a legal transaction. We must nurture our relationship with Him in order to experience the continual freedom and cleansing He provides.

In our churches, it is essential that some consistent form of discipleship is at work. We must always be learning together how to participate in spiritual disciplines (2 Peter 1:1-15). This probably will be in the form of small groups where members keep each other accountable for how they are incorporating the means of grace into their lives.

"Means of grace" is the phrase John Wesley used for spiritual disciplines. As humans we are created to live in constant abiding with God, the Holy Spirit breathing His Life into our dusty, thirsty souls (John 15:1-17). We're never intended to be able to live as Christians who are not dependent continuously on the Life of God filling us. I picture it like this: we are a dry, arid wilderness gasping for life (Psalm 143). The Spirit of God is the living water who produces health and fruitful life in that wilderness (John 7:37-39). How will He gain access to us? Will He just bulldoze His way in? No. We invite His presence into our sterile clay by "digging irrigation ditches" into which He will happily flow in gushes of refreshing life (Psalm 36:5-9). These ditches are habits of our lives which become the means. He is the grace. It's a mutual love relationship of receiving and giving. We create space for Him in our time, finances, physical well-being, and into our hearts, minds, and spirits. He pours His gracious Life into ours.

So, we gather together and ask one another how our daily, weekly habits are creating pathways for Jesus Himself to have access to our bodies, minds, hearts, and souls. We share our struggles, we pray for one another, and we cheer each other's growing successes.

The power that will result will be the power of Jesus' own holy love enabling us to love the unlovable, to humbly serve without complaining, to have willing spirits, and to forgive. That's the power and force of the grace of Jesus!

How can we continually develop discernment, fruit of the Spirit, and practices of holiness in our lives, whether it's in small tasks or in extraordinary moments?

Diane:

This will only happen through our decision to nurture the means of grace in our lives. We must develop habits that close pathways to deception and self-absorption. We must incorporate habits that open our bodies, minds, hearts, and souls to the presence of Jesus. Fasting, Bible reading, obedience, prayer, singing psalms and hymns, exercising, tithing, keeping Sabbath, reducing time on screens, fellowship with real followers of Jesus—all of these are so helpful to opening access to grace, to nurturing discernment, to bearing the fruit of the Holy Spirit, and to holy living. Begin implementing these little by little and experience the joy and freedom of being formed by His grace.

One practical way I'm learning this in my own life is by acknowledging that each moment and circumstance is infused with God's presence and ultimately with His purpose. I'm learning not to fret as much, and that I shouldn't be irritated or anxious as much. I'm practicing surrender to His purpose in every situation and gratitude for all things and all people. Just whispering, "Thank you, Jesus, for ..." lifts my heart out of myself and my eyes to my Lord. I'm walking with Him moment by moment asking Him to make me content. There is real, deep joy to be found in so-called menial tasks. To Jesus, nothing is insignificant. He can make us joyful and at peace in whatever we're doing. Have you ever met a person like this? They just shine light in darkness! That's who I want to be. Jesus, who is the Light, can fill our clay with His Light, and we will manifest His life in our bodies! What a miracle, right? That is what holiness is (2 Corinthians 4:6-10).

How can we feel empowered and encourage others to pursue holiness?

Bill:

Acts 2 gives us the most helpful outline for receiving the power of the Holy Spirit in sanctifying grace. Prayer with other believers is always necessary. We can only imagine what was talked about for the ten days between the Ascension of Jesus and

Pentecost. I am sure they rehearsed all the Spirit brought to mind of what Jesus had said about the necessity of the cross. But I am sure they also prayed for His fullness. They reviewed the prophetic promises about the Spirit being poured out upon all flesh. I cannot imagine how deeply convicted they were about how unlike the Savior they were.

But, maybe no area concerned them more than the lack of spiritual strength they possessed without Jesus and without the Spirit. Can you imagine being left with the clear command of the Lord Jesus to fulfill the Great Commission without the power of the Spirit?

As they were praying together the Spirit came. They did not dictate how He would come or what He would do when He descended. They were seeking with open hearts. They were not jockeying for position any longer. The Spirit's Lordship in each one was imaged by the blowing wind and by what seemed like individual flames of fire on each person's head.

Of those two historical events, we can surmise this from all of Scripture: the Spirit comes and goes as He wills. He is the third Person of the Divine Trinity. He is co-equal with the Father and the Son. His leading is the only source of true power. Like Ezekiel's valley of bones (Ezekiel 36), the disciples needed the animating, life-producing Wind of God breathing the only life with any redemptive power into their lives. Like the picture throughout Scripture, the Fire of God must come to illuminate every trace of sin. He must purge all yielded sins and sinfulness. And it is He who enables the Great Commission. There is no power to communicate to the nations without His touching our tongues with words that come in power, in truth, and in the Spirit (1 Thessalonians 1:5).

The encouragement of the believers began immediately. There was both preaching and testifying to the goodness of God in Christ. They came together to share meals and to study the words of Jesus shared verbally by the disciples. They prayed together and worshipped day by day. They welcomed people of different backgrounds, cultures, and ethnicities. And they were willing to be killed by the very people who planned the murder of the Son of God.

Much is said about the miracles that the Lord produced through their yielded lives. I would simply say that the redemption of Jesus is the most powerful reality in the universe. He is free, by His Spirit, to do whatever He desires. We must encourage all those on the field by showing an absolute dependence upon His redemptive power in every area of our lives, the ministries to which He has called us and to sharing the gospel. Holiness must be expressed in self-giving love. That alone is the power which is received when a person is sanctified.

If we would just follow the outline of the early church, we would be poised to both receive His sanctifying power and to build up those around us into the holy dwelling that He desires us to be for His sake and for the sake of the world.

CHAPTER 7

HOLINESS AND YOUTH

How can we explain holiness in a way a child can understand?

Diane:

First of all, we should not speak about holiness as if it is something separate and different from salvation. We should talk to them about being children who are created by God, who loves and knows them perfectly, and has made them in such a way that they will be whole when God fills their lives with Himself.

They already know they can be mean and naughty. Regularly present to them the promise from God that He can make them kind, good, and full of love. Impress upon their little hearts, according to Deuteronomy 6, that God made them, He loves them, and they belong to Him. Jesus wants the very best for their whole lives. Living with Jesus is great fun, safe for everyone, and full of adventure where they'll have to be brave and true. Goodness and love live there in Jesus' Kingdom because He is the King. Sing songs of Jesus and about life with Him. They love songs and believe the words. They'll remember them!

One of my favorite ways to teach about holiness is to give a child a lump of clay. Read Genesis 2:7 aloud to them. Talk about the intimate care God demonstrates by holding the clay tenderly in His hands, shaping it as an artist would into the shape of a human. Then talk together about what it would be like to have God hold them and shape them exactly as He desires so that they're perfect in every way (which is what "very good" means in Hebrew). Share together what it is like to have God, who is perfectly loving and absolutely the strongest, hold them up to His face and look at them in the eyes while smiling at them because He loves them so much. Then He breathes His own life into them, making them just like Himself (in His image). Have them act all of this out with their clay.

Only with His Breath (the Holy Spirit) dwelling inside them can they truly live and be who they truly are. The following is a simple way to explain it to children:

> Adam and Eve chose to turn away from God's face because they didn't trust that He was good. Can you imagine that?! They believed the lie, which caused them to not trust God's Word: "Did God *really* say …?" They couldn't receive God's Breath because they turned away from His face. They crawled out of His hands that formed them perfectly. That is called sin. It means that we want to be the boss of our lives. "We're all like sheep who've wandered off and gotten lost. We've all done our own thing, gone our own way" (Isaiah 53:6, The Message).

Jesus calls each of us to repent. That word means to turn away from sin and turn back to God. Jesus wants us to be restored to His image, to be just like Him. He says, "Come to Me! Give me all your badness. I am the only One who is strong enough to take it out of you. I can make you kind and good. I can help you obey my teachings. I can give you a heart that is clean and new, instead of selfish and mean."

The Holy Spirit of God will come and live in you if you ask Him to (Luke 11:9-13). God loves you so much and wants to make His home in you, and He wants you to make your home in Him—forever (John 14-15).

These are realities that are the essence of Christian life, which is holiness. Do not condescend to children and teach them a bunch of shallow stories. They are capable of receiving the mysteries of God; they have ears to hear. Jesus wants to call them to Himself so He can be their keeper and protect them from a life of shattered wounds. He said the Kingdom belongs to those who receive like a child.

Share with them all the beauty you know! Take them into a cathedral, let them gaze upon the altar, the stained-glass windows, the vaulted ceiling that represents heaven. Don't put them in the nursery every time; let them experience the glories of worship within the community. Let them hear their old neighbors singing with all their hearts, off-key, and look at the face of their daddy as he prays and sings. Take them to a sacred concert or dance.

Don't be "teachy." Just let Jesus speak. They can hear His whispers. If you listen sensitively, you might even get to hear from them what Jesus spoke into their hearts.

Bill:
There are five main points I think we need to convey to children. 1. *He made you for Himself.* It is always fascinating to me that the Old Testament must restore what the very first verse of Scripture makes unmistakably clear, that God is the Creator of all that is. Unless there is a line drawn between this world and the One who made it, then there is no possibility of any kind of redemption, regeneration, or sanctification. The Holy One comes to us from outside this world. He became a human being exactly as we are, but without sin. And He is available to us in divine power through the intimate comfort of the Holy Spirit. I

wonder if any biblical truth can be conveyed to our young people without a clear doctrine of creation? In this vein, it is paramount that creation be understood as a personal relationship. We are formed for an intimacy with our Maker. That is breathtaking!

2. *He is always true.* The second way I would attempt to connect a child with the holy nature of God is by pointing to His absolute trustworthiness. The faithfulness of God throughout the history of His people underscores the commitment He has to us regardless of our failures and sins. His covenantal love issues from the constancy of His own character. Nothing ever changes in the nature of holiness. He is always pure, kind, good, truthful, and He always acts with integrity. Only true holiness would leave a spotless track record of that moral and ethical consistency. The flow of revelation in Scripture shows us that our basic need is to know that God is distinct from us and knows what is best for us. I must have a sincere fear of the Lord (reverent awe) in order to properly relate to Him. He is jealous for me. He wants nothing to come between me and Him, and He will fight for that closeness even when I have betrayed Him.

3. *He is Holy Love.* Love follows creation and faithfulness because of the many ways we have corrupted the very concept of love in our day. Love must be defined by categories that are revealed, not discovered, from within our human needs. Love has to be covenantal and not bound to emotions or circumstances. That is why I think the Scriptures spend so much time early on in describing the Law (the moral instruction), so that we can learn how love acts in response to the havoc that sin has produced in every part of human nature. We need to see what holy love acts like. The moral law is the incorruptible picture of God, as Wesley famously said.[19]

4. *Jesus' message is about more than forgiveness.* I am not sure what is the most important element to clarify with so much misinformation afoot. I would think that very early in a child's walk with Jesus, the goal of a pure heart of love should be at the center of all attempts to communicate the gospel. The day I was converted, an evangelist left an indelible mark on my perception of becoming Christ's. He crossed his fingers in the shape of a cross and said as he pulled those fingers together, "He can make your will His will every time." My entire life with my Savior has seen that as the reason He came for us. He is due that kind of allegiance and He is able to produce it.

5. *He can make me like Him.* The fact that God is not bound by anything or anyone makes transformation possible. Because Christ became a human person, I am now assured that He understands all my needs and desires and is willing to come to the deepest point of corruption that my sin has produced. The Spirit comes to my mind and heart to affirm what is absolute truth, to bring peace through the atoning work of Christ, to convict me of what is not like Christ in any area of my life, and to apply to any remaining part of my life the sanctifying work that is His major role.

How is it possible to explain the Triune God to kids and new believers? They seem to understand God's individual identities, but not the "three-in-one" concept.

Bill:

I find it very helpful that you would connect the Trinity to holiness. Very few people do that and it may be one of the major reasons for our misunderstanding the biblical doctrine of holy love.

At base, we believe that before anything was created, God existed eternally. But the Bible gives us an interesting view of who God was before all that is came into existence. The Spirit hovered over the unformed materials of creation (Genesis 1:2). Because He was before all things, the Son created all that is, and it is made through Him and for Him. In fact, He holds all things together by His power (Colossians 1:16-17). In numerous places we are told that our Father God made all things (Psalm 102:25). This is important to learn. The Trinity is never divided in the work of creating and fully forming us in the image of God.

We need the Bible's revealed truth to help us place this interesting idea together. As we progress through the Word, we find that no work that God does is ever alone (John 14:6-14). All three Persons—the Father, the Son, and the Spirit—always work together. Nothing that is comes from an impersonal source. The one true God is always three Persons.

As we continue in the Bible, we find that Jesus is God the Son, who is equal to the Father. He is eternal in His sonship, and He is to be worshipped as God (Philippians 2:6-11). The Spirit is also clearly divine, eternal, and deserving of our worship (John 15:26, Matthew 28:19).

The God of the Bible is One (Ephesians 4:4-6). The only God is Love (1 John 4:8,16). Revelation indicates that "one," when applied to God, does not mean one individual thing. It refers to the unity of God (John 17:20-23). Any time a religion advocates that the term means only one person, the result is a de-emphasis on love and an emphasis on power, will, and determination. It is interesting to think about how holiness is affected by our view of the Trinity.

We have repeatedly affirmed in this work that holiness and love are inseparable. So, the direct tie between the Trinity and our lived experience of holiness are also connected. Before anything was made there were three Persons in mutual, self-giving love. That love is also holy because it is the very nature of God. So, it is crucial for a comprehensive view of holiness to always have God's love as the origin of our love. The love with which God so loved the world was that shared, personal, sacrificial love (John 3:16). The love He desires to pour into our hearts is His actual divine love (Romans 5:5). The love we are to share with one another is that love which is bestowed from the three Persons who are One in love (Galatians 5:22, Ephesians 5:22-33, 1 John 4:7-21).

How can we live out and model holiness in raising children?

Diane:

I cringe as I recall my multitude of mistakes in modeling holiness to my own kids. One thing I did right, unknowingly, was desperately need Jesus right in front of them every day. They knew how much I loved Him. They also knew what a wretch I could be, and that I apologized and asked them to pray for me. Here are some things I've come to realize over the years:

+ Don't speak badly about anyone in front of your children. Ever. Even if it's true.

+ If you're in ministry, don't complain or whine about its difficulties.

+ Don't be judgmental, critical, or negative.

+ Don't worry about money in such a way that your kids know you're stressed about it.

+ Live by faith, trusting Jesus out loud to provide for all your needs.

+ Have lots of fun together, not separated from loving God. Don't separate secular life from sacred reality.

+ Read your Bible first thing in the morning. When your kids wake up and see this happening, it will give them security and understanding of how life really works.

+ Tithe. Teach your children the joy of tithing from their own storehouse.

+ Keep the Sabbath. It's a real-life gesture of trust in God through worship and ceasing from acting like everything in life depends upon us, and not upon God. This will be a context to relieve stress and anxiety from your kids' lives.

+ Serve and love others, as an individual and as a family.

✦ Live within your means. Don't acquire unnecessary debt. Live simply, without lots of stuff. Shop at thrift stores. Wear hand-me-downs. Drive "beaters." Do this with joyful creativity. This creates a context out of which your adult children can live with contentment and peace.

After I wrote this list, I realized that each of these practical examples and exercises are actually scriptural admonitions, even straight up commands. God knew what He was talking about when He told Moses what to say in Deuteronomy 5:32-6:9. "You shall walk entirely in the way which the Lord your God has commanded you, so that you may live and that it may be well for you ..." (5:33a, NIV).

How can holiness be reflected in our parenting?

Bill:

I remember asking a mentor of mine why it was that I had no problem with the notion that the Lord could cleanse a human heart from all sin. I think I was fishing for a compliment. I thought he would say it was because I was a good biblical scholar or that I was an astute theologian. His nearly immediate response was, "Your parents." I have thought about that answer many times and I think he was absolutely right. I know we live in a time when few families are not scarred by some sort of breach in covenantal love, but I would say that the school of holiness was always intended by God to be the family.

Let me share my own experience. I would turn anyone to Deuteronomy 6:1-9 as the foundational passage for connecting parents to children (and grandchildren!) in covenantal love that is based in the holiness of God. I was raised with two parents who loved Jesus more than their children. We witnessed their obedience to His voice our entire lives. But that obedience was never bitter or servile. It always came out of a fundamental trust. We were told and shown in a thousand ways that Jesus was worthy of our trust.

We saw a pretty good balance of law and love. It is interesting that Moses makes that very point in Deuteronomy 7:7. Holiness is both a standard of righteousness and amazing love. I think that is why God desires for homes to be led by both a mother and a father. We can see the Holy One better when we know that there are rules that guide us and are couched in a heart of love.

But, far beyond every other lesson, there was the beauty of seeing two people who came from very different backgrounds work through the crucible of marriage with love always at the center. I experienced Christ-filled love through some days of radical disagreement between two opposite personality types. Holiness was the mark of their marriage. And that mutual love was extended to us and the many people who responded positively to the message of holiness in their lives.

But there is one more arena that makes family discipleship in holiness absolutely crucial. I watched the fountain of perfect love flow from within their hearts to enemies. Several times over the course of our home life, things occurred that tested my parents to the core. They were betrayed, lied about, treated shamefully, rejected, and forgotten. Did those experiences hurt? Yes, deeply. But, in the chaos, I watched carefully as the Spirit enabled two very broken people to rest upon His promises. He is holy, and those who know Him are as well. He gave His life for us when we were His enemies, and He enables that same kind of response. I witnessed that love from above (it can come from nowhere else) over and over.

So, do I think parental discipleship is key to the next generation understanding holiness in all of its facets? Without a doubt. Is it a challenge in these days of relational chaos? Absolutely. In any circumstance, if God can find the heart of a couple, a single parent, a grandparent who sees how crucial this kind of life-to-life discipleship is in the home, then there is hope, which I believe extends through generations.

Are young adults interested in holiness?

Diane:

To be given a glimpse into a life of faithfulness, loyalty, goodness, justice, and sacrifice is interesting to young adults because that is what is real. That is what they truly long for. Not virtual, violent, banal nonsense. Much of what they see and experience is just the opposite: self-centered parents, unfaithful marriages, cruelty presented as entertainment, and the prevalence of injustice in multiple areas of life. To be offered the hope of becoming the kind of person one ought to be—and living in community with others like that—is very appealing.

We must begin by cultivating relationships with them. Spend time together in non-teaching settings, listen to them, don't do lots of correcting. Have them into your home. Feed them. Let them participate in your family life at dinner, Friday night movie night with the kids, game night, family devotions. Love them. Give them a sense of belonging. Be faithful and interested in what they're involved in.

When they experience your un-fake commitment and concern for their lives, they will be interested in the God who has made you the way you are. Through your life of self-giving love toward them, they'll sense there's hope for the yearning of their soul. They'll be open to receiving the truth that God is love, deeply loves them, and longs to faithfully walk with them through every aspect of life.

If you're frantic, negative, critical, lazy, disinterested, and rude (to any person, not only to them), they'll not be open to any presentation of holiness.

In current language, we can communicate to them, "God created you. He knows everything about you, and He loves you completely. He knows your brokenness, your sin, your secret wounds, and fears. He wants you to belong to Him so He can take care of you. He will heal you, restore your life, and re-create you so that you can be the person He has always dreamed for you to be."

There are a couple things we must keep at the front of our own minds when considering how to present holiness in an appealing manner. First, holiness is the life of the Trinity—Father, Son, and Holy Spirit—in eternal relationship of mutual, other-oriented, self-offering, abiding love. Holiness is the Triune God inhabiting our bodies, minds, hearts, and souls. Every human person is created by this God, to be filled with this God. That is the essence of what makes a person whole.

So, when we consider bringing this good news to young people, we start with who God is and what His created intention is. We don't start with ourselves or with any age group as a category to approach with the gospel. We begin with the God of holy love. What is He like? What has He proven to be true about His character and work in the world of human history? What is the nature of His revelation offered to us in the Bible? Contemplating the greatness of God and His heart for all people will fill us with such joy and confidence as teachers.

Second, we must focus on who Jesus is: the second person of the Trinity, God the Son. Young generations need to be reminded of the beauty and power of who Jesus truly is and why He is essential and worth having in their lives. He is the Creator and Lord of the universe. He calms seas, heals lepers, casts out evil spirits, and raises the dead! He is the friend of the marginalized and despised, the defender of the weak. He is the One to whom they are giving their life. And that very Person is giving His Life to them!

CHAPTER 8
Holiness and Relationships

How can we be holy through our interactions with others?

Diane:

This is the essence of daily Christian living, isn't it? A very unfortunate thing about the way our Bibles are printed is the placement of chapter divisions. (Paragraph headings are even more unfortunate.) Sometimes they chop up the meaning of the whole context in a way that makes it very hard for us to gain a clear understanding. In the original texts, chapters and verses were not there. They're not inspired by God. Editors put them in. Often, they're okay. Sometimes they are problematic. Ephesians 4:1-6 should not be separated visually or thematically from Ephesians 3:14-21.

The "how" we are holy in our relationships comes from the end of chapter 3. We live a life that is worthy of our calling only by His glorious, unlimited resources, which He empowers us with in our inner beings through His Spirit. Only when Christ makes His home in our hearts, can we trust in Him and let our roots grow down deep into God's love (that's the "means of grace"). We do not have love on our own that can interact with people in a holy way. "Be completely humble and gentle; be patient, bearing with one another in love" (Ephesians 4:2, NIV). The word "love" that the New Testament uses is *agape*. It refers to the essence of who God is. *Agape* love is the Triune God—Father, Son, and Holy Spirit—who live in eternal, mutual, self-giving deference toward one another. We also read that this very Love is to fill us and enable to us to love as God does, to care more about others than ourselves (1 Corinthians 10:24).[20]

Christians don't love or live in a manner worthy of our calling or of the gospel (Philippians 1:27), like Paul is telling us to, because we've gained information about Christianity and its doctrines. Our accepting these truths to be true does not transform our lives or save us. It's a very important start! But only by receiving the presence of the Holy Spirit through surrender to Him will He pour *agape* love literally into our minds, mouths, attitudes, bodies, and hearts. The Holy Spirit transforms us into people of love (John 14:15-15;17).

> "Since you have heard about Jesus and have learned the truth that comes from him, throw off your old sinful nature and your former way of life, which is corrupted by lust and deception. Instead, let the Spirit renew your thoughts and attitudes. Put on your new nature, created to be like God—truly righteous and holy" (Ephesians 4:21-24, NLT).

We can live a life worthy when the worthy One inhabits and transforms our natures with His own. This is possible through intimate, constant dependence upon Jesus.

How can we practice holiness in our relationships with our parents?

Diane:
Personal holiness involves basic elements: love, humility, and forgiveness, to name a few. Respect and honor for our parents is a moral command. To "curse" our parents results in a death

sentence in God's Kingdom (Leviticus 20:9; Proverbs 20:20; Matthew 15:4). "To curse" means to despise, dishonor, to treat as if they are insignificant or of little esteem.

God deeply values family as the primary means of redemption for the whole world. He demands esteem for individual family parents, and for parenthood in a universal sense. Before the Triune God was any other thing—Creator, King, or Shepherd—God was Love, a Family of Father, Son, and Holy Spirit.

Regarding our own parents, we are not required to ignore the wounding and disappointment we may have received at their hands. We probably will need good counseling to maneuver through that, and our own children will as well.

But the holy life that the Triune God promises to us involves freedom. A life of holiness is one that has been set free from and healed of being curved in upon ourselves. The essence of holy love is to be more interested in the well-being of another than we are in our own well-being. Only God, who is that kind of love in Himself, can make us love in that way. Here are some things we can do:

+ We can relate to our parents with honest concern about their well-being. We can tenderly communicate with them, listen to them, ask Jesus to make us aware of and care for their needs. We can make personal sacrifices to make them feel valued and safe. We can love as Jesus loves—putting others ahead of ourselves.

+ The way we speak about our parents is significant. Are we speaking about them to others in ways that are disparaging? Belittling? Jesus promised that every word from our mouths will be judged (Matthew 12:36). Where does that get us, anyway? Speak to Jesus about these things that are challenging regarding our parents. He's the only One who ultimately can do anything about them, and He can heal us and set us free.

+ In humility, we can acknowledge the fact that we don't have any idea what their lives truly were like as we were growing up in their home. We can humbly submit to the unknown. It wasn't and still is none of our business. Humility will allow us to enter the past with the Spirit's vision, revealing the multitude of loving, sacrificial things our parents did do for us, did do right—things perhaps we were too immature, selfish, and arrogant to even notice, or maybe still are.

+ Forgiveness is not optional in Christianity. The deal Jesus gives is, "If you forgive others, I will forgive you" (Matthew 6:14-15). To be able to forgive is a major gift from God when He brings His holy presence into our lives. Just like Jesus' powerful work on the cross when He bore our sin so we don't have to carry it within us or pay its deserved penalty, He gives us power to not make people carry what they deserve to carry because of how they treated us. When we forgive, when we don't give people what they deserve, we lose absolutely nothing! To hold over someone our "being right" is a burden too much for them *and* for us.

Holiness is the power to love, be humble, and release people from their mistakes. This kind of life is available only through the Holy Spirit's presence. He loves to help you relate to your parents.

How can holiness affect daily life with family and friends?

Bill:

I believe that every facet of holiness is relatable. By that I mean, if God is working in me what pleases Him, then it will affect every aspect of my life as a person who relates.

I think the beginning point here is the awareness of the grace of holiness. This life must never be merely about me or my old patterns of relating. As a sanctified person, my heart must be attuned to others over my own interests (Philippians 2:4). That is only ever possible if He is living in me—not just a satisfied Judge or a rightful Lord but as the Love of my loves, the Desire of my desires. It is only when I am in right relationship to the heart of the Trinity that any consistent love is possible.

Let me list the areas that point me to the Holy One. These may be my areas of highest concern when it comes to the messy business of relating, but I have found in close relationships with growing saints that I am not alone. I also notice that these kinds of issues come in many of the Epistles' lists of ethical actions that are to arise from a heart that is being reformed in the image of God:

+ forgiveness from the heart;

+ discerning what is a healthy anger and that which is sinful;

+ patience, which is connected to anger;

+ lovingly risking to speak the truth in love;

+ vulnerability, teachability, and willingness to be corrected;

+ the honest expression of fears and concerns;

+ sexual purity, which incorporates a strict accountability that those close to you are clearly aware of and assured of consistently;

+ and a winsome, joyful rejection of worldliness (i.e., materialism, hedonism, sensualism, addictions to social media, gaming, virtual contexts).

In short, all the ethical standards set for the saints in Scripture are to be seen in our daily responses. Does anyone have perfect performance? No. But that heart must be willing to dive into why there is a recurrence of areas that war against the purity of our souls, and worse, affect those around us deeply. Always remember that most of this is revealed to us as we live with those who truly love us and are willing to challenge us. Without that context of growing saints, most of this talk ends up a passing fancy.

How can we introduce holiness into our romantic relationships, if it is not there yet?

Bill:

I think our response must delve into what we mean by romantic. In our day, most of the definition pertains to emotions, feelings, and actions that covertly demand that the "romancing" end in something for the giver.

Holiness touches every area of life, including our sexuality. The first hymn of praise in the Bible is Adam's rejoicing that he has been given another beautiful human who is totally different from himself (Genesis 2:23). You could say that true holiness is always romantic in the sense that a heart filled with the presence of God is always seeking the best, the highest for the other (Exodus 19:4, Deuteronomy 7:6). Unselfish love is the healthiest, most substantial, most freeing kind of love. That kind of pure love always hopes for the best in the other. It desires to pour symbols of true love on the beloved. Romance that issues from the heart of God will creatively seek myriad ways to bless, honor, exalt, and serve the other.

The Song of Solomon is the most beautiful description of romantic love in all of history. It is a remarkable description of married, sexual love based upon the gift of sex by a Creator who made us for the pleasure of total self-giving within the bonds of covenantal love between one man and one woman. God the Holy One is the author of romance. At whatever stage a person finds themselves in marriage, the bottom line should always be other-oriented love. No romantic attitude is ever truly selfless unless the Spirit of God can turn that heart and that body toward their spouse in sacrificial ways.

I remember hearing about a widow who found love notes from her departed husband that he had hidden all over the house in places that he knew she would eventually find them. She found them one by one for years. A holy romance reflects the faithful and passionate love of God. It may not be recognized or thanked, but it can be zealous at the heart level.

What joy when two hearts place the romance they desire to give and receive into the heart of the One who designed passionate love!

How should holiness manifest in our business/administrative duties?

Bill:

This directly confronts us as Salvationists because few (if any) other Christian groups or denominations have as many levels of structure and authority as we do. I am struck by how often the Epistles, when talking about holiness, start with marriage and the family and then move to business relationships. We know that Christians were the first to treat slaves as brothers and sisters. Every indication we have is that this societal shift to personal freedom, equality, and eventually more democratic societies began with the delivering power of Christ in the hearts of those in charge and those who served them. Think of the remarkable book of Philemon and its influence for thousands of years to correct our misuse of one another. Paul is clear numerous times on this front.

Those who live "over" others must treat them as equally worthy because we are all made in the image of God. Those who "serve" must honor those placed above them because God is over all structures and governments. Paul goes so far as to say we must respect them and not ever talk about those in charge with disparagement (1 Thessalonians 5:12-13).

All of us are responsible before God for how we use the status we are given. None of us is allowed to lord over another person in any denigrating way. Our mutual encouragement is the foundation of every action. To willingly treat another person as simply a cog in an institutional wheel is abominable to Christ.

The effectiveness of the Army has been one of our hallmarks. We fully acknowledge that we affirmed a quasi-military structure when we signed our covenant with God as Salvationists. We knew that to engage in the battle for human souls meant joining an Army that was comprised of warriors of love who were not preoccupied with pampered living or behaving in an overly sensitive manner. Our entire focus has always been the salvation of the person in need, whatever the cost. In such a context, there is the possibility of great abuse.

Sanctification must permeate every level of our structure in order for Jesus to be truly glorified through His Army. All of us need to constantly bring our position under the scrutiny of the Holy Spirit. If Paul worshiped the Lord who emptied Himself of anything which might grasp for Himself, then we also must be totally emptied of self.

Working under authority is one clear way to witness to the purpose of the image of God. From Eden to Paradise we are told that work is what God desires for us. We are made to be productive. No person in the Army's structure should view work as a burden. Laziness is pure foolishness and is ungodly. We must remember that we are accountable to our Lord Jesus for all that we do, say, and think. A lot of backbiting, criticism, and judgmentalism within our ranks could be dealt a death-blow if we placed ourselves under the administration of the King of Kings. Everything we do can have meaning, purpose, and fulfillment if it is done unto Him. No authority can limit the eternal productivity of a person fully yielded to the Master. Jesus was a hard worker. He loves it when we take personal, loving dominion of creation seriously.

I am convinced that we can, as a denomination, be sanctified from the ground up and from the top down. Nothing of Christ ever discounts a person, dismisses concerns, scoffs at going unrecognized, or demands advancement. The way of Christ is that of the cross every time. A spirit of servanthood must permeate our hearts, relationships, marriages, families, corps, areas, divisions, territories, and zones.

What is a healthy balance of emotions in a holy life?

Diane:

Part of being made in the image of God is to have emotion. God has emotion. Emotions are an aspect of His image which we did not lose in the Fall. But they, rather than the Holy Spirit, can become unwieldy governors of our lives. This is something we must be aware of.

A holy life is overflowing with emotion. I think entirely sanctified people might feel most passionately. Deep love and joy and appreciation are felt, and we grieve deeply over brokenness and harm. A full range of emotions is probably the most acute in a holy life. The key is that the Holy Spirit is always given access to them. He can speak to us about our anger and sorrow. He can reveal when we have moved into sins such as bitterness and self-pity. He can also reveal when we are apathetic and self-absorbed, not experiencing gratitude for the myriad good things in our lives, or when we are behaving unempathetically toward someone who is in despair. We must allow the Spirit to ignite and to regulate our emotions. But we are not to be without them.

One thing the Spirit is teaching me is to give my feelings to Him when I'm overwhelmed by them. Perhaps I've been deeply wounded by someone. That can make me swirl with confusion and negativity in my pain. So, I literally lift my hands, palms up, and say, "Jesus, I give you all I'm feeling—all my pain, anger, sorrow, sense of being rejected and unloved. This is unbearable for me. Please take all of it. I freely give this experience and how I feel to You. You are the Bearer. Only You can hold this mess. Only You are able to take it, and to heal my mind and heart. Get this off of me. I can't bear this. Set me free in Your understanding and compassionate, strong love." Seriously, if I do that and leave my emotions for Him to own and rule over, He enables me to receive peace, and even to forgive. I trust Jesus, the Lover of my soul, with my whole life.

How do we tell more resistant communities about holiness?

Diane:

Never be afraid to bring before your friends the beauty of holiness, because we must remember that this is what every human person is created for. This is what their souls are thirsting for. Even if a person sitting in the pew was dragged there by a relative or friend, the truth is that God has been pursuing them their entire lives. He wants them to taste of the mystery of His love. This vision of freedom from sinfulness, a life of blamelessness, is what they're created for. When you talk about holiness, you're partnering with Jesus by igniting in people a longing for Him.

I'll never forget the time I was leading a Bible study on the book of Colossians. I was so nervous because some people in the group were scary—very caustic, brilliant, and involved in dark behavior. I had someone read aloud Colossians 1:21-22. I was going to quickly skim across the last part: "As a result, he has brought you into his own presence, and you are holy

and blameless as you stand before him without a single fault"
(NLT). I thought it might be too much for them at this point
in their journey. But the person I was most intimidated by said,
"Wait a minute! What does this mean? What is 'blameless'?
Tell me about that. That's what I want in my life! That's what
I want to be!" She was weeping.

With joy, I explained this promise and hope for her life. Later,
I was stunned at myself. Jesus came to me with a stern face and
encouraged me to stop getting in His way by watering down
the aroma of life He wanted to present to people so that He
could allure them from death into His Kingdom of love.

How do we share holiness with new believers?

Bill:

Wesley was a wise evangelist. He knew that it was possible
to scorch the psyche and the soul of an immature Christian
and unbelievers with the message of full salvation. He advocated that there be a constant wooing of people to all that
God has for them but to do so in a way that is "drawing" and
not "driving."

I think the Bible's method of engagement is the best. I
would recommend starting with the Creation and its purpose
in humanity, noting the essence of the Fall as self-curvature
and the meaning of all salvation as being turned inside out
for others. The incarnation of Holy Love that Jesus embod-
ies should be a constant refrain—and, of course, describing
atonement as the only possible correction for self-centeredness.
It was only when God Himself did not grasp for what He
deserved that any human heart could be set free to do the same.

In essence, if the message of the Scripture is the return of God to His dwelling (our hearts), then all that is saving is holiness. We may not have to use the word, but it is definitely the DNA of all that is truly saving.

The Holy Spirit is working on every heart constantly. Prevenient grace is the call to every heart to receive the One who made them for Himself. Every step along the "order of salvation" points to the end: to become one with our God who is alone holy. What we must do is join Him in what we know He is doing and what He desires in every heart. We must always want to usher a person into His presence. We must also be very sure not to treat them with any impersonal motives.

Diane:

The first step to sharing holiness is to introduce them to Jesus. Go through the Gospels with them. Have them read aloud with you from the book of Luke. Along the way, check in with the Old Testament, showing them how Jesus is the fulfillment of the heart cries of its people, and the promises of God. Then do the same with the Gospel of John.

Clarify to them that Jesus is the eternal God. He became human, the Son of Mary. He is the Creator who has united Himself to our human nature so that He can redeem us from our sin and rescue us from our captivity to sinful nature. He sends His Spirit to dwell within our souls, minds, and bodies to cleanse us and keep us in a state of being that is united to Him, and therefore no longer mastered by sin, self, and death. These realities are clarified in the Epistles of the New Testament.

Read the Bible with them. Don't get them into other authors' writings. Feed them on the Word of God.

Never park your teaching only at what Jesus does *for* us in forgiveness. Always move to the highway of holiness—what God does *in* us. This is the way of living within this world as a member of Jesus' Kingdom.

What is your rule of thumb for when to begin having expectations of holy behaviors from people? I've heard people say, "You can't expect him to come to the altar and be a saint by Wednesday." But what should our expectations be for our children or teens, or seekers, or saints? Or ourselves?

Diane:

Holy behavior will occur only when a person lives in continual intimate face-to-face love with God. Jesus called this abiding in Him. Making our home in Him, and He in us (John 14-17).

Holiness of heart and life will only ever happen when we develop life habits that give God continual access to our beings. These are called "spiritual disciplines." I prefer what John Wesley called them, "means of grace." As shepherds and parents, our main purpose in life is helping people of every age to participate in these means as a non-negotiable part of being a human who is entirely dependent upon God (2 Peter 1:1-15; Colossians 1:24-29).

I often have thought that we stress being Christlike before people even truly know Christ, love Him, speak with Him, or listen to His Voice in His Word. If we will help our people develop disciplined lives of loving communication with and reliance upon God, then He will enter into them and transform their behavior. It will be real, not manufactured in order to outwardly impress their leaders or parents who fuss at them to do or not to do certain things.

Each individual person will grow in Christlikeness only when Christ fills their lives. And each person's growth will be at their own personal rate of speed. We must love and encourage them every step of their journey, cheering them on with great love no matter the pace.

CHAPTER 9
HOLINESS AND CULTURE

How do we teach about holiness in a world of shifting values?

Bill:

When I am tempted to lose heart amid the massive tectonic shifts in value that seem to be occurring on nearly a daily basis, I turn to Scripture. Remember that the One who inspired the Word did so in a time when there were no absolutes. The one thing about the gods of any time and place is that you cannot trust them. They are fickle, immoral, and offer no security to their believers. That is the world of the Bible. There is no place, no time in human history where you can find a God who is faithful like the God of Israel.

So, it should be of little surprise that the Holy One begins to redefine holiness from the ground up, literally. We refer to Exodus 3 because of its earth-shaking importance. Holiness as a concept had devolved, as it always does, into a mysterious, dark, and immoral thing in the hands of idolaters. God had to redeem the very term that was at the very apex of His self-revealing love. When He encountered Moses as the One alone who made the area around the burning bush holy, He immediately turned to history as the context for proof of His faithfulness (Exodus 3:6). His unwavering commitment to those who had preceded Moses provided the context for the long process of retraining His people in the meaning of holiness.

Our faith is always that—a commitment to the God who never changes in His own being and in His actions. He is always just, good, and true. He will even make covenants with fickle people, knowing full well that He will have to pay the price for their infidelity (Psalm 15:4). So, the faith we share in has a consistent historical track record of unbroken promises. Any shifting values of any time period must be viewed against that history. Change for change's sake ends up being selfishness and power in masquerade.

Everything can be made to look good or beneficial in the short term. What is truly good, truly holy, stands the test of time. We are all in a hubbub over changing values in sexuality. And we will, as a Western culture, reap the whirlwind of demanding that God's law is archaic and our experience and desires are paramount. Truth is unchanging. Untruth is constantly moving. It has to be unfixed in order to keep our attention. Truth withstands any onslaught because it is more real than gravity.

God's moral standards never change. The gospel is based on the unchanging morality of the Holy One. The message of salvation is grounded in the goodness of a God who is constantly giving Himself. His standards never change, and to attempt to alter them only brings dissolution and destruction to the culture or individuals who reject them.

We must, as followers of Jesus who are Salvationists, not cower to the ever-changing tides of values. Any dalliances with the empty promises of naturalism, empiricism, rationalism, or moral relativism will end our gospel proclamation immediately.

Teaching and preaching holiness is best offered when the basics of God's nature are emphasized without equivocation or reservation. We must never apologize for pointing to the Law and love of God. It is also imperative that we do not define holiness first by detailing the do's and don'ts of behavior. We must point to the Triune God who is Holy Love. It is that reality of mutual self-giving that precedes Creation and permeates its very purpose, including ours as humans made in the image of God. He has made us for Himself. Nothing is fully satisfying without His intimacy with us as our ultimate need. Chasing after anything apart from His dependable, constant nature ends up in a vapor. His holiness is the substance of what is real and firm and non-negotiable fidelity.

How do we stay biblical without compromising truth to be culturally relevant?

Diane:

It helps me to remember that when God inspired the biblical writers to record in written word what God wanted to be revealed about Himself to the world, nothing they wrote was considered relevant to the culture. Biblical revelation will always cut against culture. The Bible is light that penetrates into darkness. The dark doesn't want light (John 3:19-20). But we as Christians know that the God of the Bible is perfect Love, and the holiness He longs to share with us is the way to Life and wholeness. We stay biblical without compromising because it's the only sure way we have to be truly loving in the world (1 John 5:2-3).

We can remain biblical without compromising by being committed to the full authority of God's Word. This alone will give us confidence while maneuvering our way within culture. Scripture is not subject to interpretation based upon one's experiences, feelings, or the cultural mores of the current situation. Scripture interprets reason, tradition, and experience—not the other way around. We must read and listen to people who are faithful to Jesus and His Word. We must be careful to expose our minds and our hearts to teachers who are orthodox.[21] To be orthodox means to adhere to the core of agreed beliefs shared essentially by Christian traditions which accept it as true.[22] Those who dismiss the consistent and agreed upon teaching of the universal truth of Christianity since the first century, in order to present ideas and ways of living that fit in with modern culture, need to be carefully tested (1 John 4:1-6).

How do you deny yourself in a world that is pushing you to live *your* truth?

Bill:

I have often viewed the pivot of the Gospels, when Peter confesses that Jesus is the Christ, as one of the key moments in history and in theology. It is as if everything that precedes that moment comes into focus, and the result of believing in the Messiah and His purposes dictate every person's future (Mark 8; Matthew 16).

As Jesus articulates for every disciple for all time what it looks like to actually follow Him, He uses the word "deny." At the nexus of God in the flesh and what defines eternal life is the concept of self-rejection. Nothing about salvation is defined by *me*. *He* is the Truth, the Life, the Way (John 14:6). I am none of those realities. In truth, there is no such thing as *your* truth! All we can ever be are *adherents* to truth. We produce no truth. We construct no reality. We have two options with holiness: accept what is revealed or reject it. There are only two ways of living before the Holy One. One leads to life eternal, the other to eternal death.

The key to living in the culture in which truth is a supposed buffet of spiritual and ethical options is to live with a stalwart trust in the Holy One and a firm commitment to Scripture as the inerrant truth revealed. We should never claim that what we believe is "our truth," but is, instead, the best news for everyone, regardless of their circumstances. I am convinced that the very best testimony we can give is to rejoice in the truth of our revealed faith by living in it with great gratitude. If we are hostile or wavering in standards that Scripture lays out clearly, the postmodern person will pick up on indecision. They are looking for uncertainty. Misery, no matter how articulate, loves company. I don't think we know just how loving being made holy is for the person next door to us. Salt and light are necessary in a tasteless and dark culture.

How can I be sexually pure in a world that accepts and even glorifies sex and sexuality?

Diane:

These kinds of questions arise everywhere we go. They must be and can be answered in light of what holiness is. Obviously, these questions must be addressed in a full way within another context. But there are important beginning thoughts.

To be same-sex attracted is not necessarily sin. To experience gender dysphoria is not sin. To struggle with sex addiction is not sin. The way we handle these issues can either lead us to intimacy with Jesus, or to rebellion that can endanger our souls. Sin is deliberate turning away from God's design and His commands, which are always for our good, and acting out behavior that God has clarified is not His best intention for us. Our Creator loves us more than we can ever fathom. His created design for how to live in our bodies, and His ways to walk in Him, are inseparable from His essence and character of perfect love. Everything He says for us to do or not do comes from His faithful desire for our best. Sexual activity is designed and commanded by God to be participated in only within the covenant of marriage of one man and one woman (1 Corinthians 6:9-20; Matthew 19:1-12).

God deeply loves every single person. Every one of us is made for intimate belonging and union with Jesus. No person is excluded from that kind of relationship with Him. Living united with Jesus Christ is available to every human person, regardless of our sexual desires. And I might add, *especially* in light of our sexual desires. All our sexual longings are merely symbols pointing to the fact that ultimately, we are made for Jesus. All other relationships are designed to exist within that one. Jesus alone will complete us and satisfy our needs fully. For every single person, no matter our sexual proclivities, this is a Lordship issue. To live in loving, surrendered obedience to His created order will bring wholeness and joy. He created us, He loves us, and we can trust Him as we obey and walk in His ways. Our whole selves, minds, bodies, and souls were made to find their satisfaction and completeness in Christ.

How does holiness become evident in our culture today?

Diane:

The most sure way to evidence holiness in your life within our present culture is through love. By that I don't mean tolerance and sympathy. I mean biblical love, where another's life and well-being are more important to us than our own (Philippians 2:3-4). This is manifested through the way we speak, and also through humility. Our words and acts of humble kindness are key (Ephesians 5:3-4; Colossians 3:12-17).

Another major way to present holiness within culture is forgiveness. One of the most stunning things a person will encounter is witnessing forgiveness of themselves or of others who do not deserve it. When we forgive people, we are taking into our lives an evil—we're choosing not to give them what they deserve. I think the power of forgiveness is beyond any Marvel superpower, by far! Cruelty, abuse, neglect, slander, and the like can produce bitterness and resentment that have potential to destroy lives, families, institutions, and churches. To choose to forgive the evil committed against you by not giving that person what they deserve, annihilates the power of the evil. It vaporizes.

We don't pretend it never happened; we're not required to put ourselves in harm's way again. We take the hurt we've endured, and we give it to Jesus. He will most certainly bring justice. He is the only One who can (Romans 12:14-21). It's too big and heavy for us to bear. He will bear it; He's the only one who can. For people who will never admit they're wrong, this is a powerful curiosity. For people who've watched you forgive someone who'll never admit they did wrong, this is a witness to behavior that is not of this world (1 John 1:5-2:14; Ephesians 4:17-5:21; 1 Peter 3:13-18).

Another evidence is to live with biblical sexuality. It's very clear and simple throughout the Bible: sexual activity is to occur only within a faithful, monogamous marriage. There is to be no sexual activity virtually, mentally, digitally, or emotionally outside of this covenant of marriage. This commitment to holy sexuality participated in with joy and contentment, and expectation, will be the strongest witness to the goodness of a holy God. Ultimately, it is Jesus who completes and satisfies us. Our souls thirst for Him, and our bodies yearn for Him, as in a dry and weary land where there is no water. His lovingkindness is better than life itself (Psalm 63:1-8).

Our entire world is unhinged with regard to sexuality. So much harm is being done as a result. We are created to share this part of our lives within promise. To live this way is a sign for others to see what is real about the deep, satisfying love of God.

Where does entertainment fit into a holy life?

Diane:

When I think about how to deal with these aspects of life in a holy way, the word "humility" comes first to mind. Will we even entertain the concept that our entertainment *should* have boundaries? Right from the start, we must remind ourselves that to be holy innately means that we do not belong to ourselves. We belong to the One who perfectly understands the way we're made. He provides boundaries for us as a means of caring perfectly for our well-being. We will decide if He is good or not, if His boundaries are good or not. If we answer "no" to either of those, we're sunk. Holiness will not be available to us.

But if we answer "yes," God is perfectly good and loving, and so are His boundaries. Then we can look in His Word for guidance.

Scientific research shows that whatever we give our attention to, whatever we receive into our minds, will form the kind of people we will be. That's a good starting point for filtering both our time spent and the content we participate in.

I try to limit the amount of time I am on screens for entertainment like movies, shows, and social media so that my time reading God's Word is greater than my time viewing other stuff. It's very easy math. I don't want to become like social media sites, or the news, or reality TV. I want to think and respond and reach out like Christ. I want to be formed by Him.

I don't think it's super helpful to categorically say what people ought or ought not to listen to or participate in. But that also doesn't mean we can label people who offer caution on things as legalists. Let's live humbly in community and be open to input in the Spirit.

Are we using books or movies or social media as a constant means of escape or comfort? Moderation is a key factor. A little is fine. A heavy diet, not so good. Does the Lord have space in our lives to be our satisfaction? Our refuge? Or are we finding other sources more attractive?

Video game addiction is real. It is sometimes even a major cause of divorce in young couples. It's destroying the minds and futures of our children. Are we holed up somewhere in a virtual world of violence when we should be working and becoming contributing social adults? Are we glued to games on our devices when we should be giving our full faces to our children and spouse?

"The LORD examines the righteous, but the wicked, those who love violence, he hates with a passion" (Psalm 11:5, NIV). Whoa! Are we going to say weird things about God in light of this passage? Or are we going to check our hearts to see if our delight in horror movies or extremely violent shows and books might actually be wrong?

Interestingly, many Christians are scandalized by nudity and sex scenes in movies but have no problem watching people get blown to bits for a couple hours. This is not okay. Can we bring this to the light? Or are we going to get defensive and angry and shun people who question our tastes?

What about our comedy? I heard one time, "The fall of our culture began when television encouraged us to laugh at sin." Seriously, what kind of portal opens in our beings when we laugh? It could be an avenue for joy and light. But what happens when sin becomes funny?

And let's talk about pornography. The way our bodies and psyches are made, brief visual exposure to sexual activity is more instantly and powerfully addicting than crack. Visual entertainment that includes this creates desire for more. Full blown porn is easily accessible everywhere. The thing is, often times, the more one imbibes this, the more it becomes necessary to create the "zing"—it all has to get more hardcore. You get the drift. And it *is* a drift—into hellish darkness.

So, what about what you're listening to, viewing, and reading? "Mommy porn" is defined as books that are sexually explicit. Sadly, many women read these—even Christian women.

These appetites begin somewhere. A holy life will allow examination by the Lord and by others so that we're not becoming deluded fools about this stuff. It's not minor. Thankfully, the church, a holy community, is a place where these cultural realities are brought into the light and compassionately discussed together in mutual accountability. This destroys the power of shame and the lurking dominance of this kind of presence in our lives. As people who love and care for one another, we can help be a source of deliverance and freedom together in Christ.

Is reading fiction part of a holy life? Or should we only read history, biographies, travel books, theology, etc.?

Diane:

It is critical that Christians be readers. Theology, history, biographies, and relationship resources should all be part of what we regularly feed our minds. I believe it's nearly essential to also read fiction as a part of a holy life. Paul repeatedly refers to the essence of Christianity as a mystery. I don't think the depths of the beauty of holiness can even begin to be approached without imagination. To behold God, for God to behold us, is an encounter. In the still quiet of our hearts and minds this occurs, and when it does, we are transformed. Prayer is making real in our spirits and minds what we "see" in God's heart. Faith is clinging to what is unseen, and yet we know it.

Fiction provides the development of imaginative creativity. Reality is known through story. God revealed Himself and the nature of everything else, including ourselves, through story.

Fiction provides a context in which we can learn empathy. Empathy does not come naturally. One of the most powerful ways a person develops it is through story. Entering into another person's life, feeling their experience, will cultivate the ability to care about someone besides oneself.

Fiction can lift one out of their difficult context into a new world that inspires courage, sacrifice, heroism, and faithful kindness. Often, we meet characters there who are quirky, irksome, and difficult. We learn endurance and patience with these folks, perhaps learning that what is really going on in our own lives is that we are not irritated, but "irritate-able."

The Spirit convicts, then He creates mercy and grace in our attitudes.

To preachers who read fiction, I want to say, "Thank you for the depth and allure, the fragrance, the beauty—for more than mere information."

Different people's responses to what occurred at the Asbury University Outpouring in February 2023 were very telling. Where many were flocking to meet the living God who had come to love and serve and heal those hungry for Him, it seemed like others stood back with their arms crossed, demanding apologetics be taught at the altar, that people arise from prayer able to get 100 percent scores on doctrine questions. Like Zechariah in Luke 1, they demanded certainty where Mary offered herself to be beheld by her God and filled with His Life.

Perhaps we wouldn't be debating the full beauty of what God could do in our lives if we nurtured our imaginations so that His Word could fly on wind, His Spirit could make our stony hearts tender, causing rivers of living water to flow out of them. His hand can reach into our leprosy and cleanse us fully. Jesus' blood can wash away our filth. He can bear our sins in His body. He can create the world in a week, and He can instantly bring people from death to life, filling us with perfect love.

You don't believe that? You haven't experienced that? Curl up on a sofa and read *Jayber Crow*, *The Chronicles of Narnia*, *The Dean's Watch*, *The Warden*, *The Hobbit*, and *The Lord of the Rings*. The Bible is the source of all good story because it truly comes from outside this world and reveals reality. Every morning, immerse yourself within it, the very real Word of God. Yes, that's what it certainly is. Every single word is true. And yes, you can hear His voice.

Is holiness the key to revival? If it is, what will it take for churches to experience revival in today's world?

Diane:

In light of what happened at Asbury University in February 2023, we can answer this question with, "Yes, holiness is the key." If we describe holiness as Jesus does—being poor in spirit, recognizing the need for God, we will be filled. Those who hunger and thirst for righteousness shall be satisfied (Matthew 5:3, 6).

The Lord comes in reviving presence when people come to Him utterly desperate for Him, when they've stopped depending upon their own resources and come to the Source.

Revival is not an event or an "it," but the Person of Jesus coming to make His home in hungry hearts. Hunger for God is the key to revival. When we seek Him earnestly, He responds in love. When we repent, turn away from our sin, and turn to Him, He opens His heart to us. He hears our confessions of sin. He takes that sin off of us, out of us, and into Himself. He cleanses us. He fills us with His presence (1 Peter 2:24-25).

Is there a connection between holiness and justice?

Bill:

Sin and evil personally affront our Holy God. The difference between right and wrong is not a standard that the Triune God just thought up one day on a whim. Righteousness, truth, and mercy are not mere ideas or expendable measurements. They are in direct relation to the actual essence and nature of God, who is holy in all of His acts. Without this realization, it is impossible to be clear about what is right or wrong, truth or error—everything is just a fog of chaos. His nature assures us that the greatest evil will be dealt with. He provides ultimate and eternal security for us all.

When the Holy Three-in-One comes into our midst and begins to make us like Himself, we should be filled with ecstasy because His holiness offers the only chance for our crooked world to ever be made right. We are His unique actors for justice in His world!

Conclusion

Many have been tempted to think that holiness is old-fashioned, narrow, petty and, worst of all, impossible. We want to shout 'No!" Holiness is exactly what we need to understand most deeply about the God who is only Holy in Love, loving holiness. Thus, our discussions – and many debates – about holiness over the years can deflect us from the major purpose of the Holy One. His eternal plan was to involve His creatures, you and me, with His own nature. He wanted to see His reflection in us. Nothing is ultimately real without Him. He wants to bring us out of unreality (a great definition for all self-centeredness and sin) into the reality that He is.

Could it be that we in the Church are not as out of touch or irrelevant as we might be made to feel by talk of our decline in the West or our, in today's culture, increasingly strange practices and beliefs? Maybe our unrelenting focus on holiness is exactly the reality that every person is made for and needs the most! We don't mind being a bit different if someone can be touched by Jesus in redeeming power and filled with the Holy Spirit, who can only be where He can make holy. Jesus has raised us up for some reason. Perhaps pointing to – and showing how to live in – Ultimate Reality, Holy Love is that very purpose.

Our prayer is that the Holy One will be pleased to grant His favor through this book – to fulfill in you His purposes. May your hearts and minds be encouraged, and may you continue to hunger and thirst for Jesus, who has been pursuing you to belong entirely to Him your whole life. May your intimacy with God be the deepest joy of your lives.

ENDNOTES

1. Dennis F. Kinlaw, *Let's Start with Jesus* (Grand Rapids: Zondervain, 2005), 29. Diane N. Ury, "A Comparison of Abraham J.Heschel's Concept of the Sabbath as Bride and Dennis Kinlaw's concept of the Nuptial Metaphor" (Master's Thesis, Wesley Biblical Seminary, 2008), 36-38.

2. Dennis F. Kinlaw, *Lectures in Old Testament Theology* (Anderson, Indiana: Francis Asbury Press, 2010), 420.

3. Ibid, 297-315.

4. Much of what I've come to understand here about holiness is a result of the writings and teachings of Dennis F. Kinlaw.

5. Catherine Booth, *Highway of Our God* (public domain, 1882), 27.

6. Diane N. Ury, *Holy Love: Essays in Honor of Dr. M. William Ury*, "Holy Love and Personhood." Essay by Dennis F. Kinlaw (Atlanta: The Salvation Army, USA Southern Territory, 2022), pp. 2-10.

7. Diane N. Ury, editor, *Holy Love: Essays in Honor of Dr. M. William Ury*, "Holy Love and Discipleship." Essay by Nathan Doyle (Atlanta: The Salvation Army, USA Southern Territory, 2022), 87-89.

8. Dennis F. Kinlaw, *Let's Start with Jesus*, 29-31. This flow of thought is essential to understanding the nature of God's holy love and the nature of what it means for us to live a holy life.

9. Dennis F. Kinlaw, *We Live as Christ* (Nappanee, Indiana: Evangel Publishing, 2001), 39.

10. "The Hymnal for Worship and Celebration" (Waco, TX: Word Music, 1986), 92.

11. Diane often teaches about the essential nature of human beings as "hungry." We were created with need and desires that were unfallen, and therefore good. Our fallen, sinful nature has distorted our appetites. We hunger now for what will not satisfy, when in truth only Jesus satisfies our beings (Psalm 63:1-8).

12. Dennis F. Kinlaw, *Lectures in Old Testament Theology*, 444. I've heard Dr. Kinlaw speak about this fact multiple times and read of it in nearly all of his books. It's a critical understanding of the nature of God and of human life.

13. John Bright, *A History of Israel* (Philadelphia: Westminster Press, 1981). This text is an enormous help in gaining understanding of the timeline and the cultural pressures and effects of them upon the people of God throughout the history of the Old Testament.

14. James S. Stewart, *A Faith to Proclaim* (Grand Rapids, MI: Baker Book House, 1972), 128.

15. John Wesley, "Letter to Alexander Mather in 1790," in *The Life and Times of the Rev. John Wesley, M.A., Founder of the Methodists*, Vol. 3, by Luke Tyerman (Public domain, 1871), 632.

16. *NLT Chronological Life Application Study Bible* (Carol Stream, IL: Tyndale House Publishers, 2012).

17. Henrietta C. Mears, *What the Bible is All About: Bible Handbook* (Carol Stream, IL: Tyndale House Publishers, 2015).

18. Oswald Chambers, *Conformed to His Image* (Fort Washington, PA: Christian Literature Crusade, 1976), 82.

19. John Wesley, "The Original, Nature, Property, and Use of the Law," in *The Sermons of John Wesley: A Collection for*

the Christian Journey, edited by Kenneth J. Collins and Jason E. Vickers (Nashville, TN: Abingdon Press, 2013).

20. A. B. Simpson, *The Christ Life* (Harrisburg, Pennsylvania: Christian Publications, Inc. 1980), 62-63.

21. Vincent of Lerins, *Commonitory* (434 AD), Chapter 2, Paragraph 6: "… In the catholic church itself, all possible care must be taken, that **we hold that faith which has been believed everywhere, always, by all.** For that is truly and in the strictest sense Catholic, which, as the name itself and the reason of the thing declare, comprehends all universally." (The emphasis is mine. This is the long-standing definition of "orthodox belief" held by Christian traditions for centuries. Lerins wrote this to clarify how to discern between various interpretations of Scripture.)

22. Thomas C. Oden, *The Living God Systematic Theology: Volume One* (San Francisco: Harper and Row 1987), 323. "Orthodox means 'right opinion' (*orthos* + *doxa*), or 'sound doctrine,' especially religious teaching, and more particularly that teaching which holds closely to the Christian faith as formulated by the classical Christian tradition. An opinion is orthodox if it is congruent with the apostolic faith." And Thomas C. Oden, *The Word of Life, Systematic Theology: Volume Two* (Peabody, MA: Prince Press 1998), ix-x.

References

Booth, Catherine. *Highway of Our God*. Public domain, 1882.

Chambers, Oswald. *Conformed to His Image*. Fort Washington, PA: Christian Literature Crusade, 1976.

The Hymnal for Worship and Celebration. Waco, TX: Word Music, 1986.

Mears, Henrietta C. *What the Bible is All About: Bible Handbook*. Carol Stream, IL: Tyndale House Publishers, 2015.

NLT Chronological Life Application Study Bible. Carol Stream, IL: Tyndale House Publishers, 2012.

Stewart, James S. *A Faith to Proclaim*. Grand Rapids, MI: Baker Book House, 1972.

Wesley, John. "Letter to Alexander Mather in 1790." *In Life and Times of John Wesley*, by Luke Tyerman, Vol. 3. Public domain, 1871.

Wesley, John. "The Original, Nature, Property, and Use of the Law." *The Sermons of John Wesley: A Collection for the Christian Journey*, edited by Kenneth J. Collins and Jason E. Vickers. Nashville, TN: Abingdon Press, 2013.